ALASKA STEAM

SS *Victoria*

ALASKA STEAM

-A Pictorial History of the Alaska Steamship Company-

Lucile McDonald
In cooperation with the Puget Sound Maritime Historical Society

Introduction by
D.E. Skinner

Volume 11, Number 4 / 1984
ALASKA GEOGRAPHIC

The Alaska Geographic Society

To teach many more to better know and use our natural resources.

Chief Editor this issue: Jean Chapman
Editor: Penny Rennick
Editorial Assistant: Kathy Doogan
Designer: Jon.Hersh

ALASKA GEOGRAPHIC®, ISSN 0361-1353, is published quarterly by The Alaska Geographic Society, Anchorage, Alaska 99509-6057. Second-class postage paid in Edmonds, Washington 98020-3588. Printed in U.S.A. Copyright© 1984 by The Alaska Geographic Society. All rights reserved. Registered trademark; Alaska Geographic, ISSN 0361-1353; Key title Alaska Geographic.

THE ALASKA GEOGRAPHIC SOCIETY is a nonprofit organization exploring new frontiers of knowledge across the lands of the polar rim, learning how other men and other countries live in their Norths, putting the geography book back in the classroom, exploring new methods of teaching and learning — sharing in the excitement of discovery in man's wonderful new world north of 51°16'.

MEMBERS OF THE SOCIETY RECEIVE *Alaska Geographic®*, a quality magazine which devotes each quarterly issue to monographic in-depth coverage of a northern geographic region or resource-oriented subject.

MEMBERSHIP DUES in The Alaska Geographic Society are $30 per year; $34 to non-U.S. addresses. (Eighty percent of each year's dues is for a one-year subscription to *Alaska Geographic®*.) Order from The Alaska Geographic Society, Box 4-EEE, Anchorage, Alaska 99509-6057; (907) 563-5100.

MATERIAL SOUGHT: The editors of *Alaska Geographic®* seek a wide variety of informative material on the lands north of 51°16' on geographic subjects — anything to do with resources and their uses (with heavy emphasis on quality color photography) — from Alaska, northern Canada, Siberia, Japan — all geographic areas that have a relationship to Alaska in a physical or economic sense. We do not want material done in excessive scientific terminology. A query to the editors is suggested. Payments are made for all material upon publication.

CHANGE OF ADDRESS: The post office does not automatically forward *Alaska Geographic®* when you move. To ensure continous service, notify us six weeks before moving. Send us your new address and zip code (and moving date), your old address and zip code, and if possible send a mailing label from a copy of *Alaska Geographic®*. Send this information to *Alaska Geographic®* Mailing Offices, 130 Second Avenue South, Edmonds, Washington 98020-3588.

MAILING LISTS: We have begun making our members' names and addresses available to carefully screened publications and companies whose products and activities might be of interest to you. If you would prefer not to receive such mailings, please so advise us, and include your mailing label (or your name and address if label is not available).

McDonald, Lucile Saunders, 1898-
  Alaska Steam.
  Bibliography: p.
  Includes index.
  1. Alaska Steamship Co. — History. 2. Navigation — Alaska — History. 3. Alaska — History, Local. I. Puget Sound Maritime Historical Society. II. Title.
  HE633.A435M37 1984   387.5'065798   84-21673
  ISBN 0-88240-268-4

To

*the valiant men and women
who sailed the northern seas and served
ashore for the Alaska Steamship Company
and its competitors*

Contents

Foreword

The story of the Alaska Steamship Company is first and foremost the story of the people involved. There were the founders, the resourceful men and women who sailed the ships in uncharted waters in weather which at times could be as bad as any in the world, the dedicated staff ashore, and those wonderful Alaskans. Underlying all the effort of the people of Alaska Steam was one theme, service — service to all of Alaska, to its people and their every need.

The company's operation spanned the days of handling cargo piece by piece in net slings and on cargo boards to leadership in containerization, from handwritten freight bills to computerization. Operating through two world wars, through times of depression and prosperity, the company's efforts were devoted to serving all of Alaska.

We salute:

the thousands of Alaskans who rode the ships interport and to and from the Outside

the families, students and business people for whom the ships were an intimate part of daily living

the salesmen with their sample trunks, who traveled port to port displaying the newest in machinery, fashions, and everything else consumed in Alaska (Remember the Alaska Salesmen's Society, whose head officer was called the "Big Oosick"?)

the ships' crews, who were so well known

those ashore, whose tasks were vital to successful operation: the agents, longshoremen, carpenters, machinists, rate clerks, comptometer operators, storekeepers, bookkeepers and stenographers.

Technological advances, such as larger ships and sophisticated shore equipment, eventually made it impossible to serve every port, and finally the Alaska Line reluctantly decided to withdraw from the trade.

It is with great personal pleasure and a sharing in the pride of accomplishment with the family of Alaska Liners that this book is presented.

D.E. "Ned" Skinner
Seattle 1983

Introduction

The idea of collecting this company history originated with the editorial board of the Puget Sound Maritime Historical Society, which wanted to feature it in an issue of the quarterly *Sea Chest*. I had been news editor of the *Cordova Daily Times* in the 1920s, when the visits of these vessels were a regular part of the community's life, so I volunteered for the task. Plenty of former employees were willing to contribute information. After we had run several installments on Alaska Steam, the project appeared worthy of a book, especially as the Historical Society had acquired a wonderful picture collection to go with it.

Jack Dillon took over this part of the enterprise and, besides being responsible for locating suitable pictures, he furnished rare information from his private collection of maritime books and related memorabilia. A former employee of the company, he pointed out many sources of interviews and was wonderfully cooperative. I feel much indebted to him.

Not wishing to leave any stones unturned, I went north in 1975 and spent a couple of weeks doing additional research in libraries at Juneau, Sitka and Cordova. In the first library, I was intro-duced to the extremely valuable Lloyd Bayers collection of card files, albums and scrapbooks assembled by a local fish-boat captain and historian. The staff of the state library was helpful and encouraged me to put in long hours at the microfilm reader and at a special table set aside for my use.

In Cordova the museum and library were in the same building and access to old newspapers was extremely limited because of their fragile condition. The director did not wish her local patrons to see me reading the papers hour after hour, so she escorted me behind the door leading to the stacks and gave me carte blanche to read rare issues, going back to 1908. The room was cold, so I was most grateful when the head of the establishment brought in an oil heater to warm the corner where I worked.

Alaska Steam had made many friends in years past and no person turned down my requests for interviews, though in one instance I had to make a special trip to Anchorage to catch up with a former district manager.

While writing this book I have found it a pleasure to renew old friendships and record the inspiring careers of the mariners who helped pioneer the northern travel lanes.

I am especially indebted to the following whom I interviewed:

Otis Berry
Capt. Erling P. Brastad
Frank Burns
Virgil Crabb
Bill Cruchon
Capt. Adolf Danielson
Jack Dillon
Capt. Raymond Dowling
Douglas Egan
P.F. Gilmore
Sid Hayman
Capt. Ludwig Jacobson
Frank J. Kellum
Capt. Albert McCabe
H.W. McCurdy
Edward E.P. Morgan
Capt. Robert W. Nordstrom
Jay Peterson
Capt. Maurice Reaber
Douglas R. Renbarger
Robert C. Rose
F.W. Ross
Capt. Roy Selig
Capt. Homer T. Shaver
D.E. Skinner
William L. Taylor

When Robert A. Henning published a request that readers of *ALASKA*® magazine contribute anecdotes or other information about the line, a generous outpouring of recollections was received from the following:

Helen L. Ball
Harry Brewer
John E. Coulter
William E. Cruchon
R.N. De Armond
Paul T. Dodgson
Tony Dressel
Bettylee Griggs
Elisabeth S. Hakkinen
Mark Jacobs Jr.
Albert Mandle
Richard H. Meyer
W.C. Ray
Cameron A. Rich
Harold Wahlman
John L. Worthy

We also thank the many persons who generously made copies of historic photographs available to us.

Last of all, our special thanks go to Lloyd Stadum for supplying a complete list of steamships and checking this manuscript for accuracy.
Lucile McDonald
Bellevue, Washington
March 12, 1984

The story of "Alaska Steam" is, in great part, the story of Alaska. Union demands for better wages and better quarters (the ships weren't exactly "yachts"), the taking of vessels to aid the war effort in World War II, and finally, we guess, the changing times, caused the owners of the Alaska Steamship Company to cease operations. Vessels went to scrap . . . crews and office staff who had spent lifetimes with the company went elsewhere . . . and an era was gone.

Three quarters of a century of Alaska life was marked by the whistles of a long list of Alaska Steamship Company vessels. As a child of five or six, growing up in Juneau, we can remember how all we kids knew all the steamers . . . Alaska Steam . . . Admiral Line . . . or whatever . . . by their whistles. One of the old ships whose deep, resonant whistle we still recall was the *Jefferson*. We referred to her as "the old *Jeff*."

Many tiny ports that struggled and died . . . as well as some that became busy and prosperous . . . lived by the infrequent arrivals of the Alaska Steam ships. Alaskans, from the Kougarok to Ketchikan, all had to use the same ships to get "Outside" to Seattle . . . and as a result, Alaskans knew one another from one end of the Territory to the other. Sometimes it would take as much as twelve days for a vessel to make its otherwise four-day run from Seward to Seattle, stopping at canneries for canned salmon packs (husky young college-bound passengers did right well on longshore wages, helping out), at struggling mines for concentrates, at salteries and reduction plants for their season's production.

There were the traditional midnight lunches, the three-piece combos of girl orchestras . . . a violin, a saxophone, and a piano . . . and there was the skipper, popular with the ladies, who always liked the schottische, the hambo, the varsoviana, and the polkas. And there was always, in the tourist season, the last night aboard, the Captain's Dinner which was often a masquerade.

We remember Jock Livingstone, Captain of the *Northwestern* for years, who bellowed through a loud-hailer to his wife at their home some miles up-sound from Seattle that he "wouldn't be home for dinner tonight . . . loading . . ." and while we lay in Elliott Bay, off the Seattle docks, waiting for some magical hour that dovetailed with taxis or union shore gangs or something . . . the evening was lovely and soft, the last of summer, and the foredeck was crowded with Filipino cannery hands at the season's end of canning. Waiting, dead in the water, a Filipino guitar caressed the stillness . . . then another . . . and soon, a full concert of instruments and voices in song . . . foreign language unintelligible to us whites . . . but the language of happiness and day's end contentment we all felt.

Capt. Jock Livingston, on the bridge, probably was wishing he was home with his wife and didn't have to load all night.

Ouzinkie . . . Portlock . . . Latouche . . . Juneau . . . Pier Two at the foot of Marion Street . . . crowded when the boats came in . . . crowded when they left . . . Look out! That yellow cab is coming in . . .

Robert A. Henning
Robert A. Henning
President
The Alaska Geographic Society

ALASKA STEAM

Sitka during its early trading years.
Alaska Purchase Centennial Collection, Alaska Historical Library

CHAPTER 1

The Opening of the Northern Waterways

A caretaker at the old Lake Washington shipyard at Houghton, on the south side of Kirkland, Washington, spied gleaming metal in a trash heap and rescued from oblivion two bronze plaques honoring the services performed by the Alaska Steamship Company in its long career. The inscriptions recognized the firm's "significant contributions to the success of Alaska's Purchase Centennial Year" and its "first 65 years of continuous service between the Puget Sound area and Alaska and for its important contribution to the economy of this region." The callous fate to which the ornamental tablets had been consigned was as undeserved as the final destiny of the enterprise they praised.

Times have changed: the age of airlines has superseded that of steamers, ocean-going vessels are altered in character, and the great day of the passenger liner is over.

But the story should be told of the venturesome ships and staunch navigators who served the northern waterways and the vast empty lands of Alaska for a span of 77 years, from 1894 to 1971.

A veteran sea captain told me that the three most challenging pilotages in the world used to be the waters of Alaska, remote Patagonia, and the Great Barrier Reef in Australia. The passage to Alaska was the longest of these. It had narrow, winding, tide-swept channels, rock pinnacles and, in places, the additional hazard of icebergs. Gale-swept open seas had to be crossed in winter and those vessels penetrating beyond the Aleutian Chain risked the arctic ice pack. Before the 1870s, Alaska's coast was shunned by all except a few hardy explorers, whaling captains and sealers. A few venturesome traders opened stores in the southeastern part of the Territory and an occasional fur company vessel or revenue cutter anchored in the harbors. Accounts of travelers invariably spoke of the ship lying off Hoonah or Wrangell in southeastern Alaska, and described the transport of goods ashore in Indian canoes or small boats.

Alaskan shores were inhospitable,

uncharted and subject to gales and treacherous tides. A company would have to have a pressing reason for inaugurating a steamship line to a region which offered such barren promise.

Nonetheless, regular boat service from U.S. ports to Sitka began in 1867, following purchase of the Territory from Russia and the dispatch of occupation troops. Sailings out of Portland, Oregon, were monthly. They carried north a motley assortment of speculators and fortune seekers. Within another two years a considerable number of vessels were also departing from San Francisco. Eight ships left there in March 1869, carrying cargoes of assorted merchandise. During the first nine years that the Americans were in Alaska, letters were delivered no farther north than Sitka. In time, establishment of a mail route became urgent, and in 1870 a mail contract was granted.

In 1875 the Oregon Steamship Company took over the mail contract and remained alone in this trade until 1881. Then the Pacific Coast Steamship Company of San Francisco began running the *Ancon*, the *Idaho* and later the *Eureka* to southeastern Alaska once a month. Quite a few pleasure travelers discovered that this route possessed some of the grandest scenery on the continent. The steamers started from Portland or from San Francisco, adapting their schedule to cargo demand and emergencies. Generally, a vessel would clear from Puget Sound ports during the first days of each month, stopping in Port Townsend and Victoria to take on mail and freight. The arrival date at these two cities was a matter of guesswork and usually one did not expect the boat until she was within sight. A traveler might have to wait a week for

Native canoes lightering supplies ashore at Wrangell in 1883. This illustration first appeared in *Leslie's Illustrated Newspaper* on Feb. 3, 1883.

**Houses of the Russian-American Company
located on the shore of Unalaska Island.**

THE *IDAHO* SEIZED

On her last trip from Sitka down the *Idaho* reached Port Townsend on the afternoon of December 24. It was intended to have her leave for Portland sometime in the night but upon inspection by the customs officers a quantity of opium was discovered in the kitchen, secreted there by the Chinese cook. The latter was subsequently arrested and held to answer by United States Commissioner (James G.) Swan in the sum of $50. Twenty pounds of unstamped opium was found in the room of the ship's carpenter, Charles Foster, who was also tried before the commissioner and held in the sum of $100. These seizures led to a general overhauling and inspection of the cargo by the entire customs force and an additional force from the revenue cutter *Wolcott.* The search commenced late on Saturday night and continued through the week unceasingly until Thursday. Quantities of opium were found scattered among the cargo throughout the vessel, a great deal of it being packed in barrels which were stowed among other barrels of oil. Several hundred pounds were found in the engine room and it was thought that considerable more of it was thrown in the furnace and burned up. The greatest difficulty was experienced in searching among the coal, there being some 400 tons on board. A gang of laborers was employed and every part of the vessel was thoroughly searched, bringing a hundred parcels to light each day. Under the boilers four or five pounds were found. Among a lot of old junk a number of cases of Irish whiskey and several cases of champagne were unearthed. It is impossible to tell exactly how much opium was obtained, as no official information can be had. Guesswork places the amount at from 500 to 1,000 pounds. It is perhaps the largest seizure ever made in the Puget Sound collection district. For a long time it has been suspected by the customs officers at Port Townsend that large quantities of opium were taken to Portland on the *Idaho*, but the manner in which it was done left no clue for the officers to work on. She was closely watched on her last trip from Portland to Alaska and that some opium which has so far been found was tracked by the officers, it is said, from the Chinese houses in Victoria direct to the *Idaho* before she left for the North last December.

The suspicions of the customs officers were first excited by the frequent trips ashore of the Chinese cook who was hiding the opium under the ample folds of his celestial cloak. The *Idaho* was detained altogether a week at Port Townsend and was only suffered to depart after a bond in the penalty of $10,000 was given to answer such legal proceedings by libel or otherwise as might be taken against her. Captain Waterbury, inspector of customs, having resigned, there was no inspector on board the ship on her down trip and the smugglers took immediate advantage of it.

Newspaper clipping from Jan. 21, 1881, issue of *The Alaskan*

SS *Idaho*
Puget Sound Maritime Historical Society

passage. In midwinter, departures were arranged "so as to have the light of the full moon in northern ports, where the sun sets at three or four o'clock on December afternoons." The *Idaho* regularly announced her impending arrival by firing a cannon on the way in.

An extra feature of the *Idaho*'s return voyage might be the visit of a squad from a revenue cutter to search her hold. Members of the crew were not above smuggling opium. On one trip in 1881, several hundred pounds of the drug were hidden in barrels in her cargo and under the boilers.

The presence of gold in Alaska had been known since the days of Russian occupation, but prospectors were slow to penetrate the land of long, dark winters in search of the precious metal. Some persisted and the Alaska Commercial Company, which bought out the Russian trading posts, and the North American Transportation and Trading Company followed the fortune-seekers into the Interior, erecting trading posts in far-flung sections of western Alaska, and operating boats to serve them.

Gold mining began at Juneau; in 1880 there was a strike. The Treadwell Mine was opened soon after. Other discoveries followed at Forty Mile Creek in 1886, and at Sunrise in 1894.

A romantic memory survives of two early Pacific Coast Steamship Company steamers, the *Idaho* and the *Ancon*. The early-day side-wheeler *Ancon* must have been quite a sight as she picked her way through northern waters. The ship had been built on the East Coast in 1868 and had a walking beam. The company stressed her fine staterooms and table accommodations and the scenery of unsurpassed grandeur through which she passed. Cabin rate was $30 to Sitka; steerage was $15. Stops were scheduled at Wrangell, Juneau, Killisnoo, Tongass, Naha, Kasaan, Taku, Glacier Bay and of course the capital, Sitka.

Journeys in Alaska, a book compiled from newspaper columns and published in 1885, told of cruising on both the *Idaho* and the *Ancon*. The author, E. Ruhamah Scidmore, spoke of living on the steamer three or four weeks and feeling the ocean swells only while crossing short stretches of Queen Charlotte Sound and Dixon Entrance. She described stopping at Victoria, where the steward purchased his last fresh supplies.

> It was within half an hour of sailing time when the herders drove the sleek fellows [cattle] down to the wharf and for an hour there was a scene that surpassed anything under a circus tent or within a Spanish arena. The sailors and stevedores had a proper respect for the bellowing beasts and kept their distance, as they barricaded them into a corner of the wharf... The crowd gathered and increased, the eighty passengers disregarded all signs and rules, mounted on the paddleboxes and clung to the ratlines forward, applauded the picador and matador and hummed suggestive airs from Carmen.

Calls on the Inside Passage to Alaska were at clusters of bark Indian huts, tents and a new wooden house or two. Canneries always had Chinese and Indian workers. There were salteries, each shipping 500 to 1,500 barrels of fish in the summer. Wrangell Narrows, although used by Natives and Hudson's Bay Co. traders, was not considered a safe passage (Capt. George Vancouver had not explored it). The USS *Saginaw* had made a survey in 1869, and in 1884 Captain Coghlan of the USS *Adams* sounded and marked the channel with a few stakes and buoys, but no complete charts existed.

The big attraction on the round-trip was a visit to one of the glaciers, usually Muir or Taku, where passengers were often permitted to go ashore. Scidmore wrote about the stop at Taku Glacier.

> The passengers put on old clothes, got into the small boats, and were rowed within 100 feet of shore. From that point they were taken off one by one in the lightest boat and carried the last 20 feet in the sailors' arms through sinking mud and water. The burly captain picked out the slightest young girl and carried her ashore like a doll; but the second officer, deceived by the hollow eyes of one tall woman, lifted her up gallantly, floundered for a while in the mud and the awful surprise of her weight, and then bearer and burden took a headlong plunge.
>
> The passengers trailed along like so many ants across the sandy moraine... stumbling over rocks and pebbles and jumping shallow streams. They mounted 500 feet or more to a spectacular viewpoint, where they sat on rough boulders and munched soda crackers from a brown-paper bundle. They walked to

other scenic spots and frolicked until it was time to wade through mud ankle-deep and be carried back to the boats. The receding tide had obliged the sailors to push the boats farther off. When one frail boat was about full there was a crash, an avalanche of ice went splashing into the sea from the smaller glacier up the bay, and a great wave curling from it washed the boat back and left it grounded. Men without rubber boots were then so well soaked and so plastered with mud that they just stepped over the boat's side and helped the rubber-clad sailors float it off. The lower deck and engine room were hanging full and strewn with muddy boots and drying clothes all day, and the stewards were heard to wonder what great fun there was in getting all their clothes spoiled, that the passengers need take on so over a glacier.

By 1885 the Pacific Coast Steamship Company had developed considerable summer tourist trade to Sitka. In 1886 it put on the *City of Topeka* to serve more southeastern Alaska ports and carry the mail. She was replaced at intervals by the *Mexico.*

In 1892 the Pacific Coast Steamship Co. was offered more competition when Capt. David Morgan had the *Chilkat* constructed at Astoria, Oregon, for his cannery work and then had her rebuilt with passenger accommodations. She took travelers at rates lower than those charged by Pacific, thereby cutting into that pioneer firm's revenues.

Alaskan travel picked up. Eighteen hundred tourists visited the Territory during the summer of 1892. So much interest was shown in the new country that members of most excursion parties returned home and publicized their impressions in local newspapers.

In the spring of 1894 Pacific Coast added the *Queen* to its fleet, with accommodations for 250 first-class passengers from San Francisco and Port Townsend. "She is unexcelled by any vessel for speed, elegance and comfort," pronounced the *Juneau Mining Record.*

Later that same year, the company overhauled the *City of Topeka*, installed electric lights and enlarged the steerage in anticipation of a heavy spring migration.

More menacing to the Pacific Coast line than the competition offered by the little *Chilkat* was the threat from a new quarter.

In December 1894, a group composed of Charles E. Peabody, Capt. George Roberts, Capt. Melville Nichols, George Lent, Frank E. Burns and Walter Oakes incorporated the Alaska Steamship Company in Port Townsend. It was capitalized at $30,000 in 300 shares of $100 each.

Peabody, who headed the new company, was born in Brooklyn, New York, in 1857. He was the son of a master for the old Black Ball line, which ran from New York to Liverpool. The young man completed his education in a German university. He was employed first on Wall Street, then went into an unsuccessful farming venture in Minnesota. In 1882 he was appointed special agent for the Treasury Department, with headquarters on Puget Sound. He resigned to become a cashier of the Ladd and Tilton Bank in Port Town-

send, then left that position to take over operation of Tibbal's Wharf in the same city. He was to become prominent in marine transportation, but his initial effort was represented by a very modest craft.

The founders of the Alaska Line looked around for a ship with which to begin their service and found it near at hand. The *Willapa*, a wooden steamer owned by the Hastings Steamboat Company, was then running to Neah Bay. Launched at Astoria on June 15, 1882, she began her career as the *General Miles* of the Ilwaco Steam Navigation Company, and began the passenger run between the two lower Columbia ports in Washington and Oregon. She frequently made the trip outside the river mouth with merchandise for South Bend and Oysterville, returning with oysters for transshipment. She also carried military supplies for Fort Canby and, at night, towed log rafts to the Astoria sawmills.

In a few years branch railroads made inroads into the navigation company's rich territory. The *General Miles* was sold in 1889 to the Portland and Coast Steamship Company, which lengthened the craft and renamed her the *Willapa*. She ran to Grays Harbor and Coos Bay until she was brought to Port Townsend. She made her last trip between there and Neah Bay on Nov. 13, 1894, then her new owners reconditioned her for the Alaska trade.

In her original role as the *General Miles* the steamer had been 100 feet long. Remodeled, her dimensions were 136 by 20 by 10 feet. A newspaper story said that $15,000 was spent to put her in condition for the northern run, adding, "People are surprised at the transformation on the

upper deck where there are 14 large staterooms, each with two beds, some double with spring mattresses. Each room has a portable washstand in the corner, also easy chairs." On the upper deck were a smoking and card room and a ladies' social hall. Below was a dining hall with eight staterooms on either side. The galley was forward, next to the engine room, and beyond that was the steerage. In between was space for livestock.

Advertisements announced that the *Willapa* would leave March 3, 1895, on her first trip north and depart from Seattle every 16 days thereafter.

George Lent, in an interview, declared war on the Pacific Coast Steamship Co., which had dominated the northern waterways for so long.

"The monopoly is about to be broken," he announced. *"For years Pacific Coast has carried freight from San Francisco to Alaska at a lesser rate than from Puget Sound, and now the merchants of that area have taken the matter in hand and are demanding the same rates as their California rivals. We propose to have all freight landed at Puget Sound points and shipped east over local roads instead of sending it to San Francisco and then east, as the Pacific Coast Steamship Co. has been doing, to the detriment of home interests.*

"If any benefit is to be derived from the change, [Puget] Sound merchants will receive it. Myself and partners are steamboat men and are in the business to stay. [George Lent and George Roberts

had been on the *City of Kingston* on Puget Sound for years.] *We hope to revolutionize steamboating on the Alaska route."*

Residents of the Territory regarded this development with undisguised interest.

"This new line seems to be a puzzle to the Pacific Coast Steamship Co.," the *Alaska News* of Juneau commented, "as a number of Northern Pacific Railroad officials are interested in it and it is a well-defined rumor that the railroad company is behind the enterprise, which of course makes it a very different proposition from fighting a small corporation."

In reality the new line was independent, but its officers may have cultivated friends in railroad circles because the Northern Pacific would naturally profit from the channeling of business to the Northwest. In fact, one of the founders, Walter Oakes, was son of the president of the New York railroad.

By Feb. 26, 1895, the *Willapa* was already reported to have a full cargo booked. The new company opened offices at the foot of Union Street at Schwabacher's Wharf in Seattle.

Consternation reigned in the headquarters of the Pacific Coast Steamship Company as its officers observed the efforts of a determined rival. Other small enterprises had never been able to cut in on the noncannery business in southeastern Alaska. The stream of miners bound for the Canadian Yukon was increasing and it had looked as though Pacific Coast was to be richly rewarded for pioneering the route. Now this outsider came, offering attractive accommodations and undercutting prevailing prices. Acting defensively, Pacific Coast reduced

its rates sharply, bringing down the first-class fare from Seattle to Juneau from $52 to $20. Second-class tickets were dropped from $30 to $10, and the freight rate was cut to $3 a ton.

The Juneau newspaper gleefully heralded the freight rate battle, noting in late February, "The *Chilkat* met the cut by a rate of $16 and $8 but since the increase [the *City of Topeka* upped its price of cabin passage slightly to $25] it raised to $20 and $10. When the *Willapa* commences to run, Pacific Coast Steamship Company is likely to cut fares in two to $10 and $5. When that happens it will be cheaper for our residents to travel on the boats than to stay at home and board or batch."

This prediction was very close to realization. On the day after the announcement that the *Willapa* had a full cargo for her maiden voyage North, Pacific Coast once more slashed its rates on the two vessels ready for early departure, the *Al-Ki* and the *City of Topeka*. Pacific would carry first-class passengers to Wrangell for $10 and steerage passengers for $5. Rates to Juneau would be $12 and $6; to Sitka, $15 and $7.

"We will carry people to Alaska for nothing before we will let the opposition boats do any business," Superintendent Johnson of Pacific Coast declared. "We have operated our steamers on the Alaska route at a loss and as soon as we succeed in building up a paying business someone else jumps in and tries to take our profits."

The agent for the rival *Chilkat* responded in print, "We can stand the freight cut rates as long as they can."

A fresh rumor in the battle was that Pacific Coast might bring in still another

◀ **SS Queen**
Puget Sound Maritime Historical Society

steamer, the *Coos Bay*, to start at the same time as the *Willapa*.

"In that event," gloated the Juneau editor, "residents may have the unique spectacle of a steamboat race up Gastineau Channel twice each month, and be afforded the opportunity of making bets on the probable winner. The old days of the Mississippi River races between the steamers *Robert E. Lee* and *Natchez* are likely to be reproduced in all their intensity and excitement upon the waters of this northern sea."

The *Post-Intelligencer* in Seattle predicted that a battle royal was to be expected when the *Willapa* made her appearance. It was announced that she would go through to Chilkat, sufficient business having been offered. This had not been one of Pacific Coast's calls.

On March 3, 1895, the *Willapa* sailed without mishap, carrying 79 passengers, 23 horses and several sleds for a mining party stacked on the deck's upper works. Capt. George Roberts, in command, brought her into Juneau, where passengers reported their accommodations were good, table and service excellent. Local businessmen were not pleased to learn that she was going on to deliver 572 parcels at Chilkat and 190 at Dyea, for they insisted Yukoners ought to outfit in Juneau, not Seattle.

George Lent, the boat's chief engineer, told everyone his company did not intend to be scared off by Pacific Coast and would give that firm all the competition it wanted, even if the *Willapa* was smaller than the rival's ships and the opposition was a big concern.

The new company showed more courage than the owner of the *Chilkat*, for that same day her captain spread the word around Juneau that this was the vessel's last trip for the time being, $500 having been lost on the voyage.

The rumor breezed about in Juneau that when the *Willapa* returned from Lynn Canal, the Pacific Coast faction would block her from taking passengers south. This did not seem to deter her. She picked up 40 tons of ore from Sheep Creek and was back in Seattle by March 18.

The *Willapa*'s second trip to Alaska was eventful. During most of the passage to Juneau she was in a snowstorm and experiencing heavy seas. One evening the lights of St. Elmo's fire were visible at the masthead and the wire cable connecting the two masts appeared studded with balls of fire. On the return trip she stopped at least a dozen times to avoid running into icebergs ten feet in diameter and eight to ten feet high. On a dark night 50 miles south of Juneau she collided with one iceberg at 11 o'clock and slightly damaged her stem. After returning on April 3 with thirty tons of fish and eight passengers she had to be put on the beach at West Seattle for repairs.

Peabody had gone north on the *Willapa*'s second trip to discuss freight and passenger rates with Juneau merchants. He promised that for the rest of the year the steamer would not run to Chilkat, and that no goods would be brought by the crew to be peddled around town in competition with local businesses. He also made a sporting pledge to deposit, in a bank, 25 percent of all freight receipts, which the company would agree to forfeit if the boat did not stay on the run a year.

The *Willapa* survived the season's hot competition. In October, Peabody again reminded Juneau merchants that it was time to renew or cancel their contracts. He published this statement in the *Alaska Searchlight*:

Through whose endeavors have you received unprecedented rates from Pacific Coast Steamship Company and how long will they last if your citizens are not inclined favorably to Alaska Steamship Company? Is it for love of development of Alaska that they have established the present rates, or is it to kill off all hope of an established opposition and thereby ensure themselves a monopoly, such as they have controlled, for another term of years?" He concluded, *"Trusting you will see it to your advantage to divide your business between us for the year 1896.*

The two shipping lines were well aware that they were competing for something big. Contrary to the general impression about Alaska prior to the great days of the 1898 gold rush, throughout 1895 and 1896 mining news was trickling in from scattered parts of the Territory. Parties of prospectors passed through Juneau bound for a gold discovery at the head of Cook Inlet; other men were searching for

The SS *Willapa* was the first ship of the newly organized Alaska Steamship Company. Her first sailing for Alaska Steam was March 3, 1895. On March 19, 1897, during her third year of service with the line, she was cast ashore on a reef near Bella Bella, British Columbia, and abandoned. She was later sold to Canadian Pacific, who refloated and repaired her. She met her end by burning in a fire boat demonstration in Seattle harbor on Aug. 19, 1950.
Joe D. Williamson ▶

gold on the Copper River. The citizens of Juneau were extremely skeptical of the goings-on in the "Clondyke." (The name probably came from mispronunciation of an Indian word, *thron-dak*, meaning "plenty of fish.") In late 1896, when news of the winter's cleanup of gold reached the papers, they became as excited as those readers in the States would be later.

During the winter of 1896 the Alaska Line struggled to hang onto its slight gains. Peabody, visiting Juneau again, appealed on behalf of his company saying, "No greedy stockholders were waiting for great profits."

Throughout those first two years the *Willapa* managed to leave Seattle every 14 days. The local papers were still interested in the race between the individual vessels. Once they reported the *Al-Ki* overhauling the *Willapa* on Milbanke Sound on the trip south, after the *Willapa*

had five hours' head start from Juneau. Another time, in November 1895, the *Searchlight* said, "The *Willapa* passed the *City of Topeka* at Sumdum on the last trip down, but was overtaken and passed before Wrangell. Just as the *Topeka* was leaving Wrangell wharf the *Willapa* arrived. She again passed the *Topeka* while that vessel was in Ketchikan and cleared from Mary Island three hours before the *Topeka*, but was again overtaken and passed before reaching Milbanke Sound." One can almost hear the passengers cheering the winner of each lap.

The Pacific Coast Steamship Company eventually placed four vessels in Alaskan service: the *Queen*, the *City of Topeka*, the *Al-Ki* and the *Mexico*. In August 1897, a traveler reported, "The *Mexico* followed the *Willapa* around, stopping at the same landings and leaving when she did." The

Mexico undercut the *Willapa*'s fares, but the sturdy competitor kept in the race. The *Willapa* obtained a contract to carry mail on her twice-monthly trips. In July 1896 she survived a near accident. Fifty miles south of Nanaimo she ran onto a rock at low tide, stopping so suddenly that the passengers were alarmed. The ship lurched to starboard, but Captain Roberts righted her. After hanging up for two hours, she floated off with the tide. In the interval, a passenger played the violin to calm the others. The *Willapa* had to go into dry dock to repair the damage before her next trip north.

After the gold strike of 1896, boat transportation to Dyea, or later to Skagway at the foot of the Chilkoot Trail, had become so cheap that a steadily increasing stream of prospectors poured into the Yukon.

◄SS *Willapa* at Juneau in 1897.

and one half Tons of Gold, Bricks and Dust
... Alaska Commercial Co's store in Dawson June 9 ...

CHAPTER 2

Gold Rush Days

On July 17, 1897, the steamer *Portland* came from St. Michael at the mouth of the Yukon River, bringing a ton and a half of gold. The precious metal had traveled down the Yukon on the stern-wheeler *Portus B. Weare* of the North American Transportation and Trading Company. The treasure was mostly in nuggets, showier than the pokes of dust that had arrived in the past.

As one sourdough remarked, "We knew there were furs and fish and gold up north, but we were as surprised as the greenhorns back East to read in the papers that at Dawson you could go out and pick up big gold nuggets just lying on top of the ground."

The rush to quick wealth began immediately and steamship competition was a forgotten issue. Not enough vessels were available to carry the crowds. Many a decrepit and unseaworthy craft was

◀ **Gold, one and a half tons of it in bricks and dust, in the Alaska Commercial Company's store in Dawson, June 9, 1901.**
Puget Sound Maritime Historical Society

pulled out of retirement, refitted, and hastily placed in service.

The *Willapa* participated in the rush. On one trip north, 25 dogs belonging to Yukoners were on board. Four of the animals got loose, panicked, jumped overboard and were lost.

Alaska Steam could no longer keep its promise to the Juneau merchants. Like the other lines, its boat was routed directly to Dyea, bypassing Juneau. It was not long before disaster overtook two of the competing vessels, the Pacific Steam's *Mexico* and *Willapa*.

On March 16, 1897, the *Willapa* departed from Schwabacher's dock in Seattle with a great flurry, taking every passenger who possibly could be accommodated in berths or on the floor of the bunk room. Several crowded aboard at the last minute without having bought tickets. One passenger wrote home, "We are sleeping in all kinds of positions and places."

Two nights later, while battling heavy gales at Dixon Entrance, the steamboat ran up on Regatta Reef. Passengers abed at the time did not feel the blow. The stern was swept windward by the storm, then the *Willapa* listed to one side and was left well up on the reef. Captain Roberts hoped high tide might carry her off, but the seams opened and water rushed into the hold. The pumps were useless. Lifeboats were launched and the passengers and provisions were taken a mile and a half to Campbell Island.

Next day the crew worked at removing freight and baggage. They shot several horses that had to be left in the hold. Fierce winds continued to batter the vessel and she parted amidships. It was late afternoon before a southbound steamer, the *Barbara Boscowitz*, conveyed the passengers to Bella Bella. The company chartered the steamer *Edith* to bring everyone to Juneau. Yukoners aboard mourned the loss of their outfits.

Alaska Steam had difficulty in finding a replacement for their staunch little ship. The company had to take daily operational costs into consideration. The *Willapa* had averaged less than $80 in daily expenses. The company had to find another vessel which combined economy of operation and carrying capacity. They settled on the *Alliance* and chartered her until they purchased two other vessels.

Efforts to float the *Willapa* were to no avail that spring and she was abandoned to the underwriters. In June, when the weather was more favorable, a wrecking crew was able to float her off. The salvagers found that Indians had been there ahead of them. They had wrenched off doors, taken out sashes, taken bunks and mattresses, cut out moldings and electric fittings, taken away gaffs, booms, ropes, bell, whistle and railings. Nevertheless, the engine and boilers functioned. The *Willapa* was brought to Victoria,

where she was repaired and then run on the west coast of British Columbia until 1902.

That redoubtable craft, the *Willapa*, had made a name for herself. A Juneau merchant probably was not far wrong when he declared, ''I venture to say that the *Willapa* was responsible for seven-eighths of the Alaskan business that came to Seattle before and at the beginning of the gold rush.''

After the *Willapa* ran aground, Alaska Steam chartered the *Rosalie*, a wooden propeller steamer, for two voyages with an option to buy. She was 136 by 27 by 10 feet, built in 1893 in Alameda, California. She had been on the San Francisco-to-Oakland run as a ferry 18 months before being purchased for the Alaska trade. She left on her initial trip north May 12, 1894, for the Northwestern Steamship Company, but after two voyages to the Territory she was put on the Seattle-Victoria route. She was sold to Alaska Steam in 1897. The *Willapa*'s former officers, Captain Roberts and Chief Engineer Lent, took charge of her. A better substitute for the *Willapa* would have been hard to find, for the two vessels were approximately the same size. Some alterations were made when Alaska Steam bought the *Rosalie*; the dining hall, which was also the social hall, was moved from the passenger deck to aft of the main deck and 10 additional staterooms adjoining it were built. The passenger deck had 14 staterooms and a smoking room forward.

An account of traveling in the *Rosalie* comes from Capt. Homer T. Shaver, who, as a small boy, sailed on her to Skagway in 1899. He described how crowded she was, not so much with prospectors as with people going to establish businesses.

Many of the men were in a gambling mood. They would draw a chalk line on the upper deck and throw silver dollars toward it; the one who pitched his coin nearest the line took the pot. Young Homer was paid for chasing the coins that started to roll overboard and he accumulated $40 of his own before the boat pulled into Skagway. A dock had been built there by that time, but when the tide went out it left the *Rosalie* sitting on the mud flat, with the wharf about twenty feet above her deck, Shaver related.

By the end of 1897, $4 million worth of gold had been landed in Seattle and 8,000 men had outfitted in the city and gone north. The following year, 1898, was a frenzied one. The flow of wealth from the Yukon prompted the opening of an assay office in the Puget Sound city. Boats were brought from every available source and pressed into service to transport the gold-hungry men.

At the other end of the run, at the head of Lynn Canal at Dyea, the port for the Klondike, no wharves existed and there were none of the customary means of disembarking. Horses were dropped into the sea and forced to swim toward land. Baggage intended for lighters often fell into the surf. Provisions were strewn along the beach and some passengers had to wade ashore.

Little has been written of the courage of skippers who piloted those heavily laden passenger steamers, many of them not more than 150 feet in length, through reef-strewn channels, into fog banks and under stormy skies. They were navigating on the tops of sunken mountain ranges where uncharted pinnacles thrust

SS *Portland*▶

SS *Jefferson* at Skagway.

The freight yard on the beach at Dyea.

unyielding summits close to the surface, and where great tides raged through narrow passages, creating foaming overfalls.

Buoys and other aids to navigation were lacking, and maps were poor guides to the perils concealed along travel routes. A captain learned by experience. If trouble occurred he had no radio with which to call for assistance. When he had to put passengers and crew ashore he contended with chilling temperatures.

The scenery along the gold rush waterways of the Inland Passage was magnificent. Snow-covered peaks lined the eastern horizon, forests clothed the lower slopes; but the waterways were lonely, little traveled except by other vessels returning southward. In the vastness of the landscape any venturesome steamboat was isolated, far from villages and from today's comforting sights: fishing fleets, tugs with barges in tow, loggers and pleasure craft.

If one scans the Seattle newspapers published toward the end of the century, one finds mining news as much a daily feature as the modern stock-market page. At least three columns daily were given over to the latest developments in the great search for precious metals in Alaska and the Pacific Northwest. In the depths of a nationwide depression, the lure of quick riches offered hope to many. Fantastic stories emanated from the North. Outfitters advertised all sorts of free advice to prospectors. In Seattle nearly an

◄ The SS *Dora* was referred to in her heyday with the Alaska Steamship Company, the period 1910-20, as the "Bulldog of Alaska" for her ability to handle the fierce conditions of the Gulf of Alaska, Shelikof Strait and water surrounding the Aleutian Islands.

entire page of each day's newspaper was devoted to announcements of steamboat sailings to Alaska and ads for the White Pass and Yukon Railroad after it was completed. Vessels regularly mentioned in the scheduled sailings were the *Rosalie, Farallon* and *Humboldt*, which served the ports of Juneau, Dyea and Skagway for such independent firms as the Washington and Alaska Steamship Company and the West Coast Steam Navigation Co. The steamship lines boasted six trips monthly. Sandwiched between the advertisements were announcements concerning the *Dora*, which the Alaska Commercial Company ran from Juneau to Kodiak, and the *Excelsior* of the Pacific Steam Whaling Company, which covered the territory between Juneau, Yakutat and points in western Alaska.

Juneau became a thriving center of commercial and mining activity. Ten years earlier the town had been an area of thick brush, stinging devil's club and a few scattered log cabins. It was visited only by the *Ancon* and *Idaho*, which might bring 15 passengers during the whole winter. Now, Juneau's citizens were happy to see eight steamers in port in one day.

In the winter of 1897, as a temporary measure, the Alaska Line joined forces with the Washington and Alaska Steamship Co., each contributing a boat to the Skagway run. The *Rosalie* and the *City of Seattle* alternated each week with sailings from the Northern Pacific dock in Tacoma and Schwabacher's in Seattle. By July 1898, the Alaska line had chartered a second ship, the *Dirigo* (which they purchased later in 1899). It was said that Alaska Steam made enough money out of the *Rosalie* to buy the *Dirigo* outright,

SS *Dirigo*

SS _Farallon_

secure a controlling interest in the _Farallon_, which had been competing in the gold-rush trade for West Coast Steam Navigation Company, and help with the purchase of the _Dolphin_, the next addition to the company fleet.

The _Dirigo_ was a steam schooner built at Hoquiam. She was 165 feet long, with a beam of 35 feet, a depth of 13½ feet and 843 gross tons overall. Immediately after completion she was placed in the Alaska trade by J.S. Kimball and Company. She was noted for her hard luck. In April 1898, she left Skagway and put in at Juneau because of condenser troubles. When she tried to come alongside the steamer _Czarina_ at Peoples Wharf, her engine room signals got crossed and she rammed the other vessel, badly holing her side. The _Czarina_ had to make a quick run for the beach at Douglas.

On March 9, 1899, the _Dirigo_ was stranded with 100 passengers aboard off Midway Island, south of Juneau, during a heavy snowstorm. She was on the rocks for 46 hours before she was refloated. She was commanded by two well-known officers, Capt. George Roberts and Chief Engineer George Lent. On March 12 the _Dirigo_ was towed to Juneau and was later brought to Seattle. She was so badly damaged she required a new keel and garboard strakes. Repairs ran to about $30,000, more than a third of the vessel's value. Eventually Alaska Steam had her back on the run with the _Rosalie_ on a regular schedule.

The _Dirigo_ figured in a more cheerful news story the same year. The Oct. 18, 1899, edition of the _Seattle Post-Intelligencer_ described her return to Seattle with the largest single shipment of gold up to that time sent by way of

Lynn Canal. The metal was valued at more than $1,064,000 and weighed two tons. It consisted mostly of gold bars, melted at Dawson, which were enclosed in wooden boxes bound with steel. Two officers of the North West Mounted Police accompanied the consignment; all together there were six armed guards standing six-hour watches. Also on board were two leather trunks containing $90,000 in gold dust from one bank and another box containing $37,000 shipped by the Alaska Commercial Company. The vessel also brought 7,500 cases of canned salmon and 78 passengers on that trip.

The _Farallon_ was the fourth vessel acquired by Alaska Steam. A wooden steam schooner of 749 gross tons, she was built in 1888 in San Francisco and operated in competition with vessels of the Pacific Coast Steamship Co. on the Alaska run. For several years after 1898 she was placed on the Seattle-Skagway route by Dodwell and Co. Her story emphasizes the hazards of navigating northern waters before they had been charted. After she went to Alaska Steam, the records show that in July 1899 she ran onto rocks near the Canadian Pacific Wharf at Wrangell. In November of the same year, she lost a propeller blade to a rock in British Columbia and had to be towed south by the tug _Pilgrim_. On Dec. 23, while she was discharging freight at Seward, a sudden northwest storm sprang up, damaging and nearly sinking the _Farallon_. Before she could clear the dock, she wrecked it and further damaged herself.

Amid the excitement of the Klondike stampede those two dogged competitors,

The _Seward_, _Victoria_ and _Dolphin_ at dock.

the Pacific Coast and Alaska Steamship companies, prospered. By 1899 the old higher rates had again been put into effect for freight and $32 was quoted as the first-class passenger fare to Skagway. For the time being there was enough business for all and the earlier cutthroat rivalry ceased. In a short time six companies combined to raise the rates even higher and the fares became $40, first class, and $25, steerage. Then, too, interest was high in copper discoveries on the islands of Prince William Sound, at Copper City on the Tonsina River and at Lituya Bay.

In the summer of 1900 the press carried stories of a new 1,500-ton steel, twin-screw steamer purchased by Alaska Steam. She was built in Wilmington, Delaware, christened the *Al Foster*, and used as a club boat to carry fishing parties on Long Island Sound. When she was brought west around Cape Horn she became the *Dolphin*. She measured 225 feet long, with a 40-foot beam and a triple-expansion engine.

Her voyage to the Pacific Coast started out uneventfully. She made a fast passage from Point Lucia in the West Indies to Montevideo in 21 days, then trouble began. Off the Plata River she encountered a severe storm. While she was anchored at Tierra del Fuego the crew had a confrontation with the inhabitants, who tried to burn the vessel. Then another unfortunate incident occurred when a steward stirred up a mutiny. By the time the *Dolphin* arrived at Coronel, Chile, to take on coal, authorities had to be appealed to for help. Six mutineers were left behind in the local jail. The remainder of the *Dolphin*'s voyage was without incident. She put in for a week in San

Francisco for overhauling, then continued to Puget Sound to begin the Skagway run.

The company heralded the *Dolphin* in its advertising as speedy and elegantly fitted up, adding that she was prepared to handle rapid, limited express service, "perishable and fast freight only." She was equipped to carry 150 first-class and 200 second-class passengers, and 600 tons of cargo. At first her master was Capt. John A. "Dynamite Johnnie" O'Brien who had brought her around the Horn. A courageous Irishman who had gone to sea on sailing ships as a boy, he was a pudgy man, five feet, four inches in height, quiet-voiced, smartly dressed, and he looked anything but a hero. He became one of the company's most famous skippers. He was identified with the *Dolphin* only a short time. Within a year Capt. George Roberts took command of her; he was later succeeded by Capt. J.C. Hunter.

In 1898 the Pacific Coast Steamship Company, not to be outdone by its smaller rival, built a new vessel in San Francisco, the *Senator*. A big tourist season was anticipated because so much space had been devoted by newspapers to the gold rush, and the scenery of Alaska had become well known. As a fresh attraction Pacific Coast offered a thirty-day excursion to Nome by way of the White Pass and Yukon Railroad. With this railroad line to the Interior completed, the port of Dyea on Lynn Canal was doomed. Everything was moved to the rail terminal at Skagway; even the piling from the wharf was taken up and carried to the boom town next door. The public had almost forgotten that only three years before, many were not thinking of the Alaskan route to the Yukon, but were trying to reach Dawson and the Yukon in a round-

about manner — overland by the Edmonton Trail through Canada.

Thirty thousand white men were now in Alaska, compared with four thousand before the gold rush began in 1897. Even a small company like Alaska Steam could afford to operate several ships. Though Klondike prospecting was tapering off, mining firms were moving in, buying up good claims and dredging for gold. Machinery to thaw frozen soil permitted work to continue year-round, despite the usual autumn exodus from the goldfields. In the fall of 1900 departing miners filled every available berth southbound; beds frequently had to be made up on a ship's dining tables and in the social hall.

A typical news dispatch, Oct. 16, 1901, describes the arrival of the *Dolphin* from Lynn Canal with 211 passengers and $750,000 in gold. Some large lots of gold, worth $304,000 and $120,000, were consigned to banks and shipped in charge of the Alaska Express Company. One passenger came aboard with $18,848. Others brought pokes of gold dust and nuggets ranging in value from $500 to $8,000.

Faster than some of the other plodding vessels on the northern run, the *Dolphin* was frequently reported racing her rivals. In March 1901, a most exciting contest with the *Victorian* from Skagway and Juneau was reported. The ships left at the same time. "For 41 miles," the report said, "the *Victorian* was in the *Dolphin*'s smoke. At Berners Bay the wind died and it was *Victorian* weather. *Dolphin* no longer had the lead and *Victorian* came into Juneau half an hour ahead of her."

On another occasion the *Dolphin* raced

SS *Dolphin* at sea.▶
Puget Sound Maritime Historical Society

the *City of Seattle* 800 miles from Vancouver to Skagway. Most of the time they were within sight of each other; they were abreast for eight hours while going up Lynn Canal. The *Dolphin* finally pulled ahead and won by half a mile. It must have been a thrilling spectacle to see those two steamboats chuffing up that frigid channel lined with snowcapped peaks and glaciers. Competition of this type furnished the sporting news for sourdough readers.

With the *Dolphin*, Alaska Steam made its first decisive bid for an active role in the tourist trade. It had experienced less expansion during the gold frenzy than any of its contemporary lines, but now the company could solicit some travelers bent on pleasure; Pacific Coast had dominated the tourist trade for too long.

Ships braving the Alaskan seas were an essential lifeline to Alaska. Boats were late if the weather slowed the trip. The *Valdez News* once complained when the *Excelsior* was eight days overdue. There was no means of receiving word about her whereabouts. The town was in danger of running short of essential provisions. "There has been no fresh meat for nearly two weeks and the run on salt meats has caused a shortage of that article. Potatoes and other items are scarce also," the *News* complained. In Skagway there was much worry and telegraphing south to find out when the *Dolphin* would leave Seattle with the mail. Sometimes the *Dolphin* arrived from the south covered with ice from bow to stern. On one occasion the *Dirigo* was carried backward, like driftwood, in a storm on Lynn Canal until her skipper realized that he had no choice but to seek refuge until the wind went down.

Plans for building 14 lighthouses in Alaskan waters were discussed. They were much needed, particularly in winter when days were short. In May 1901, the announcement came that the first beacons would be built at Five Fingers, 77 miles below Juneau, where the *Dirigo* had suffered $35,000 in damage 18 months earlier.

For a time in the summer of 1903, Alaska Steam carried enough passengers to justify chartering the *Humboldt*, which since the summer of 1899 had been publicized by a competing company as the "Alaska Flyer — 65 hours to Juneau."

In 1904 the *Dolphin* was temporarily withdrawn from Alaskan service and for a brief period took the place of the *Clallam* on the Victoria run, after the latter's tragic sinking in the Strait of Juan de Fuca.

The *Jefferson* was another company vessel built after the bloom was off the southeastern Alaska trade and gold mining had shifted to Nome and other westward regions. In 1904 she replaced the *Humboldt*. The new steamship was the first vessel exceeding 1,000 tons for Alaska Steam; she was one of only four ships expressly constructed for Alaska Steam during the company's long history. She measured 207 by 39.8 by 25.6 feet, and weighed 1,615 tons. She was driven by single screw, with a triple-expansion engine and three single-ended Scotch boilers. The *Jefferson* was constructed of wood by the Heath shipyard in Tacoma and named after Jefferson County, where the company president, Charles E. Peabody, had resided. She was launched April 2, 1904. Her captain, J.G. "Gus" Nord, had one of the longest careers as skipper in the Alaskan maritime service. A picture of her social hall exists, a narrow corridor with a single row of wicker armchairs lined along one side, a companionway at the end leading to two upper rows of staterooms. On the wall in a prominent position was a sign, Gambling Prohibited.

On Nov. 23, 1904, during the *Jefferson*'s first year on the Alaska run, she was beached at Sheep Creek in Gastineau Channel with a broken propeller. Her freight was transferred to the *City of Seattle*, which in turn hit a rock near Amalga Landing and had to be beached also. Sailing the northern seas was not a business proposition for the fainthearted.

◄The SS *Jefferson*'s comfortable onboard social hall.
Puget Sound Maritime Historical Society

Lighters were used to bring supplies ashore during the early winters at Nome.
Joe D. Williamson

CHAPTER **3**

Copper Riches

For several decades the mineral riches of the North continued to be a key factor in the fortunes of the Alaska Steamship Co. At first the gold of the Klondike sustained the flow of traffic and assured boat service by competing lines to the ports of southeastern Alaska. Meanwhile much had been happening on the Bering Sea side of the Territory. Some of the output of the Yukon valley had come downriver on steamers and trade had been lively at St. Michael. Gold was being prospected here and there in the Interior when, suddenly, in the fall of 1899, spectacular finds were made in the sands of Cape Nome. They were reputed to be the richest of all in what was considered poor men's country, because it cost little there to take out the gold. During the first season, the latter part of 1899, working the beach and camping in tents, 2,000 men and women extracted between one million and two million dollars worth of metal. A new gold rush was launched, and the trading and transportation companies already active to the Westward gained some rivals.

Among the newcomers was the Northwestern Commercial Co.; it was founded by John Rosene and a group of Seattle businessmen including J.D. Trenholme, Moritz Thomsen, George T. Williams and Frank Hofius. They opened a large store in Nome and organized a lighterage firm to discharge cargoes in the shallow roadstead. In 1904 they purchased three vessels for the Nome run, the *Victoria, Olympia* and *Tacoma,* and formed the Northwestern Steamship Company. The three vessels had been sailing between Tacoma and the Orient under the flag of the Northern Pacific Steamship Copany, an offshoot of the Northern Pacific Railroad. Originally the trio had been British vessels, but during the Spanish American War a special act of Congress permitted them to be placed under American registry. The *Victoria* began the Nome run in the summer of 1900, then after 1904, during the winter, she filled in on the southwestern Alaska route.

The next few years saw other financial manipulations during which the Pacific Steam Whaling Co., owner of canneries and ships, was absorbed by a new con-

Gold bullion worth $1,250,000 in the Miners & Merchants Bank, Nome, June 10, 1906.

cern, the Pacific Packing and Navigation Co. This company failed in 1904. Three of its vessels, the *Santa Ana, Excelsior* and *Newport,* went to Capt. E.E. Caine of Seattle. He formed the Alaska Pacific Navigation Company, which also purchased the *James Dollar* and rechristened her the *Santa Clara.* The *Newport* was placed on the mail route from Valdez to Unalaska; the *Santa Ana* and the *Excelsior* ran between Seattle, Valdez and Cook Inlet. The *Newport* was later sold and replaced by the *Dora.* On Jan. 1, 1905, the Alaska Pacific Navigation Company disposed of its fleet to the Northwestern Steamship Company. Northwestern, in addition to the Nome service, took over the route to Valdez, where a boom was in the making.

In 1905 the Guggenheim-Morgan interests were ready to do something about exploiting the copper deposits they had acquired on the Copper River, a tributary to Prince William Sound. A mess of clams dug on the beach of Latouche Island had led to the discovery of low-grade ore in 1897, and the staking of a prospect close to the shore by J.K. Beatson. Beginning two years later a little copper was mined and shipped from the island. Not much attention was paid to it, nor to another deposit at Ellamar, for the great magnet was still Klondike gold.

The upper reaches of the Copper River basin are divided from the Yukon by a range of mountains. It was assumed that gold prevailed in the western as well as in the eastern valleys. Some of the prospectors found their way to Prince William Sound, intending to go into the Interior via the Copper River. The region around

SS *Santa Ana* amid the ice floes.▶

the sound had been almost unexploited, although the Russians had once maintained a fur trading post on Montague Island. In 1899 Louis Sloss and Company of San Francisco built the Pacific Packing Company cannery at the head of Odiak Slough on the south side of the present city of Cordova. Four years later Pacific Packing joined the Alaska Packers Association and operated until 1905. The Pacific Steam Whaling Company erected another cannery close to the Odiak establishment at the same time. Both companies had tramlines (a system of open wagons drawn on tracks) to bring fish from the Copper River by way of Eyak Lake. In the spring of 1895 the Pacific Steam operation moved to Orca, about three miles north of Cordova, and there a post office was established in 1900.

The passenger vessel operated by Pacific Steam Whaling Company, the *Valencia,* brought some gold prospectors to the area. Entry to the Copper River country through the river mouth was extremely difficult. Many who tried to go in that way were disappointed in trying to cross glaciers and rugged country on foot, and came out complaining bitterly about their suffering.

An easier route to the Copper River country was from Valdez, though it involved hiking for days over a formidable glacier. As a consequence of the Klondike flurry in the winter of 1897, a tent city had sprouted on the beach at the foot of Valdez Glacier. Rumors were flying that the country was lined with gold. Thousands of prospectors arrived and packed their supplies into the Interior by a perilous

◀ **The original Valdez townsite, with glacier in the background.**
P.S. Hunt

route, which never achieved the publicity accorded the Chilkoot Trail out of Dyea and Skagway. To accommodate the flood of gold seekers, a post office was established at Valdez in 1899. An easier trail leading inland was hacked out over Thompson Pass and along the Lowe River, where crude bridges were placed over small streams. (The present Richardson Highway succeeds this early trail established by government surveyors.)

While gold was the prime objective of the roving hordes penetrating the Interior, the country was suspected of having an abundance of copper. Although the Indians in the area possessed many copper objects, large deposits of the ore were not found until late in the summer of 1900.

A group of prospectors known as the McClellan party agreed to go through the Copper River country, breaking up in pairs to explore the possibilities of the entire area. Toward the end of the season two of them, Jack Smith and Clarence Warner (assigned to the Chitina River, a tributary of the Copper), were in despair; they had run short of grub and one had sprained his ankle. As they rested by a stream they spied a patch of green on a nearby mountain. They were skeptical of its significance until one of them picked up a piece of rock from the stream. It was mineral-bearing and showed a silvery streak when broken open. The pair gathered more samples, thinking the streak was silver. Gradually they worked up the mountain to the green spot, which turned out to be a copper outcrop — pure chalcocite. They did not learn what it was until several weeks later, when they showed samples to a Geological Survey expert.

The two men staked a number of claims before going to Valdez to rejoin their companions. There they met Stephen A. Birch, a mining engineer who was exploring for himself and some New York investors, including J.P. Morgan and Simon Guggenheim. He arranged to take an option on their discovery for an agreed price. Next year he returned, confirming the find to be all that Warner and Smith had said it was. These claims became the site of the famous Kennecott Copper Mine. Kennecott ore was high grade; some of the rock almost pure copper.

Some of the original party of 11 prospectors had been grubstaked by other mine investors, so there were altogether 32 claimants to the mine. The purchase, arranged by Birch, resulted in lawsuits which dragged through the courts for five years before development of the property could begin. Birch needed financial aid to exploit the deposits. As a result Morgan and Guggenheim organized a syndicate known as the Kennecott Copper Corp., named after the glacier adjacent to the mining property. The syndicate prepared to build a railroad to bring ore down to Prince William Sound, and sought a means of transporting the copper from there to the company-owned smelters in Tacoma, which had been established in 1890 to handle lead, gold and silver reduction. In 1902, copper reduction facilities were added and by 1905 the copper refinery was in operation and receiving ores from the Kennecott mine.

The Morgan-Guggenheim syndicate's first step toward solving maritime transportation problems was to secure control of the stock of the Northwestern Steamship Company. The syndicate also purchased some of the canneries of the

Kennicott, Alaska

Cameron

defunct Pacific Packing and Navigation Company. Next it bought the collier *Edith* in San Francisco and the steamships *Saratoga, Orizaba* and *Yucatan,* which had been Ward Line boats in the Cuban fruit trade. Other purchases were the passenger ship *Pennsylvania,* the ore carrier *Seward,* built at the Moran yard in Seattle for the Northwestern Steamship Co., and a large passenger ship, the *Oregon.*

In 1908 the syndicate was ready to start construction of the Copper River and Northwestern Railroad to its copper mines. On January 1, it completed a merger of marine transportation lines to Alaska. Alaska Steam was consolidated with Northwestern Steam, forming a new Alaska Steamship Company under Nevada laws. Charles E. Peabody, a minority stockholder, became the firm's president for the first two years. Altogether, the company controlled 15 steamers; a total of 28,160 tons, the largest fleet of its kind operating exclusively to Alaska.

There was a strong reason for Alaska Steam's acquiescence to this changed state of affairs. The gold rush had subsided and while there were still northbound cargoes to Alaska, little was available to fill holds on the southbound voyage. Copper ore was seen as supplying this bulk, helpful also as ballast for crossing the stormy Gulf of Alaska and, of course, for bringing in revenue. The cargoes would come not only from the rail terminal at Cordova (which grew out of the original settlement, Odiak, or Eyak), but also from Latouche, where the syndicate had bought out Beatson and begun shipments in 1910.

Much drama was involved in construc-

The freighter SS *Seward* unloading construction materials at Cordova.
E.A. Hegg photo, Alaska Historical Library

◀**An early view of the mine at Kennecott.**
Guy F. Cameron

The 1907 storm that smashed Katalla.

tion of the Copper River and Northwestern Railroad. For a time it was not known whether the most important port would be Valdez, where the government had located the terminus of a telegraph line and a road to the Interior, or Katalla or Cordova. Katalla seemed to be winning. It had two assets: coal was discovered there in 1896, but the extent of the field was not known for several years; and oil was found in 1894, though no one paid much attention to it at the time.

Around 1907, at the height of competition, Katalla had a population of seven thousand, three docks and thirty-seven saloons. It lacked a good harbor, although a breakwater was attempted. A terrific fall storm smashed the port installations, reducing Katalla to a ghost town. After that the storm barrier construction centered on Cordova.

Building a railroad line to the Interior was a tough proposition which involved crossing the moraines of glaciers. Michael J. Heney, the engineer who succeeded in carrying out this difficult project, began in January 1906 by building a wharf and a trestle approach at Cordova. He leased the abandoned cannery buildings on the slough where there was an ideal site for shipping yards. In the fall of the same year the syndicate purchased Heney's enterprise, but it was October 1911 before the final spike in the railroad was driven.

All of this activity focused attention on Prince William Sound, because ship transportation was needed for workers and materials for the railroad. The new wharves at Cordova and at Kodiak were the only two in all of Alaska above the level of the gulf. The Cordova wharf had a capacity of 10,000 tons, and was 725 feet long by 80 feet wide. At low tide there was 35 feet of water. Vessels arrived with more merchandise than had ever before been received in that part of Alaska. It was nothing for a ship to unload six flatcars of lumber, coal and cement — all for the railroad. On one day the *Seward*, *Yucatan* and *Santa Clara* might be discharging cargo at the same time.

The newly consolidated Alaska Steamship Company operated four routes: Seattle to Skagway, Seattle to Seward, Seattle to Nome, and the mail run from Seward to Unalaska. At first vessels bound for Prince William Sound followed the outside route from Seattle, but Captain Peabody altered this in 1909 and directed all vessels to use the Inside Passage.

Great expansion took place under the Morgan-Guggenheim syndicate. The old Alaska Steamship Co. had been operating from the Northern Pacific Pier 1 in Seattle; the Northwestern Steamship Co. had used Pier 4, the Arlington Dock. Now both of these locations were abandoned. The Northern Pacific enlarged Pier 2 and, early in 1909, the Alaska Steamship Co. moved to offices at its shore end.

Alaska Steam had brought into the new company the *Jefferson*, *Dolphin*, *Farallon* and *Dirigo*. Northwestern Steam had contributed the *Dora*, *Edith*, *Orizaba* (rechristened *Northwestern*), *Olympia*, *Pennsylvania*, *Santa Ana*, *Saratoga*, *Santa Clara*, *Seward*, *Victoria*, *Yucatan*, the gas schooner *Oakland*, and the famous sailing ship *St. Paul*. Peabody adopted his family house flag for the line — a black ball centered on a red flag. (After his retirement the flag was modified to include an A across the black ball and a white rim between the ball and the red field.)

Railroad builders at Cordova, November 1908. Front row, left to right: James English, track superintendent; Mr. Van Cleve; Sam Murchison, superintendent of construction; Michael J. Heney, contractor; Capt. John J. O'Brien of Alaska Steamship Company; E.C. Hawkins, chief engineer; Alfred Williams, assistant chief engineer (on step); Dr. B.F. Whiting, chief surgeon; P.J. O'Brien, bridges. Rear row, from left: Dr. W.W. Council, assistant surgeon; Archie Shiels, supply; Bill Simpson, steam shovel; Mr. Robinson, two unknowns.

CORDOVA, ALASKA. OCT. 1909.

In 1910 George Peabody resigned and Joseph H. Young, general superintendent of the operating department of the Southern Pacific Railroad, was brought from San Francisco to succeed him and also become head of the Copper River and Northwestern Railroad. S.W. Eccles was vice-president. Later Young moved the office to the Lowman Building. Here Capt. D.H. Jarvis, who acted as personal representative of the Guggenheim interests and treasurer of the steamship company, also had his headquarters. Another occupant of an office in the same building was C.A. Sprague, who was brought from Utah and made assistant purchasing agent. His title applied not only to the steamship company, but also to the Katalla Company, the Kennecott mine and other allied enterprises.

No longer were the steamship passenger lists dominated by brawling sourdoughs. Now passengers were men and women who had made their stake, professional people, tourists and others from a more prosperous layer of society. In 1909, the year of the Alaska-Yukon Pacific Exposition in Seattle, the company arranged special excursions and featured, as a fresh attraction, a trip up the railroad from Cordova to view Miles and Childs glaciers. This tour also afforded glimpses of the railroad construction and of Camp 1, where the railroad was feeding a thousand workers. On one trip the *Ohio* delivered 1,324 sheep to supply fresh mutton to the camps.

That same year the National Editorial Association came up on the *Northwestern*, saw an Indian village, viewed the glaciers, and made a trip to a coal mine. At Valdez, a ball was given for the visitors.

◀**Cordova in the fall of 1909.**

Unloading a steamer at Cordova.

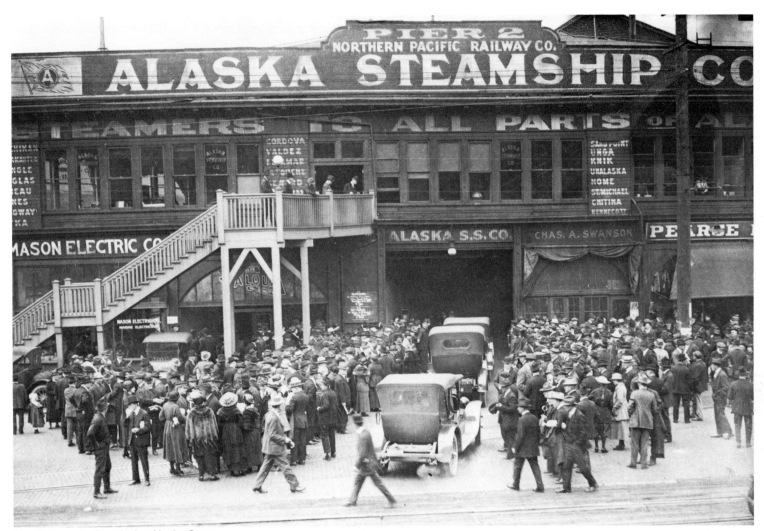

Pier 2, home in Seattle for Alaska Steam.
Joe D. Williamson

◀**The docks on the Seattle waterfront.**
Puget Sound Maritime Historical Society

This is the view an Alaska steamer had as it approached its moorings in Seattle.
Puget Sound Maritime Historical Society

By far the greatest fanfare made was over the arrival of a party of financiers in July. The *Yucatan* was fitted in palatial style. Brass beds were put in some of the staterooms. Extra baths were installed, the observation room was given plate-glass sides, new dining tables were added, as well as green plush cushions and draperies, three large cold-storage rooms and a large ice machine. When the vessel reached Cordova bringing nineteen company officials, five steamers were in port discharging railroad material. The next call was at Seward to inspect other rail activity. After that the *Yucatan* took her moneyed passengers on to the Bering Sea.

Now that the company's boats were of deeper draft than the earlier vessels, they encountered unknown rocks that were often named for the vessels striking them. Navigation to the Alaska coast continued to be hazardous. This was a condition the company could not remedy, but it did continue improving the steamers. Radio telegraph had been perfected about the time of the merger, and an arrangement was made with the United Wireless Telegraph Co. to rent radio equipment and obtain operators for the fleet.

When Alaska Steam's vessels began calling at ports in Prince William Sound, it added to the itinerary the perilous crossing of the stormy Gulf of Alaska. Lack of a beacon at the entrance to the sound was remedied in 1909 with construction of a lighthouse on Cape Hinchinbrook. Even with this additional light, however, the *Victoria* grounded years later near the promontory when Capt. Charles S. Davis was on watch. The light was thought not to have been working at the time. The ship was able to back off, her bow badly damaged. She transferred her passengers to the *Bertha* and proceeded to Cordova.

Some of the vessels which changed hands did not remain long in the company. On March 20, 1908, the *Saratoga* was wrecked on Busby Island, near Ellamar on Prince William Sound, during a snowstorm. The crew and passengers, 118 persons in all, were taken to Valdez in small boats; the ship was a total loss. In May 1909 the *Pennsylvania* was sold to Pacific Mail. The following October the *Santa Clara* went to a company operating between Portland and San Francisco.

The *Ohio*, bought in July 1908, was wrecked Aug. 26, 1909, in Milbanke Sound with a loss of four lives. Under a full moon in a smooth sea, she struck a reef in Hie-kish Narrows north of Bella Bella. She almost made the two miles to Carter Bay before the boilers exploded. She went down fast. Of the 219 persons on board, four were lost. Some of the passengers panicked and jumped overboard. For hours, lifeboats searched for them. The survivors, many scantily clad, were taken to Swanson Bay in two small steamers. Michael Heney, the engineer of Copper River fame, bought up all the available clothing in the settlement and gave it to them. He himself lost a shipment of railroad ties, rails and 35 horses. Purser Fred Stevens, the quartermaster and radio operator, died while attempting to save a seasick soldier who had remained in his bunk.

In September 1909, the Moran shipyard delivered to the company a new oil-burning freighter, the *Latouche*. She was put under the command of Capt. John Livingstone. The ship had a well deck to carry lumber cargoes, and was extremely useful in delivering construction materials, locomotives and railroad cars at Cordova. When she was no longer needed for this purpose her well deck was built up flush with the fo'c'sle head and afterhouse, making her suitable for cannery cargoes.

The winter of 1909-10 was a bad one for the company. The *Farallon* replaced the *Dora* on the westward run during a brief period when the *Dora* was in Seattle for an overhaul. She left Valdez on Jan. 2, 1910, for Unalaska. A passenger had asked to be put off at Iliamna Bay with gold-mining equipment intended for a new location in the Interior. Captain Hunter had never been to that area. On Jan. 5, light snow sifted down as he was about to have a boat lowered to set his passenger ashore. Although it was high tide the ship ran onto a rock.

Soon after the *Farallon* struck, the strong Cook Inlet tide began to ebb. The stern and bow sank until they tightened and broke guy lines on the smokestack and other fixtures on the upper deck. The ship rested high out of the water and rolled heavily. Planking gave way and everyone took to the six lifeboats, which were quickly filled with provisions and some coal for fires. The small craft picked their way through slush ice to the shore. As soon as the boats were unloaded the crew went back and salvaged canvas and other supplies for building shelters. In temperatures below zero, with ice and snow all around, it was imperative to make as snug a camp as possible. No radio was then in use and there was very little chance of being rescued quickly. Next day several boats went out to the ship again and brought back doors and lumber for building huts. Provisions were ample, but

Captain Hunter on the bridge.
Puget Sound Maritime Historical Society

no wood was available except for willows dug from the snow. High winds prevailed at times and the thermometer frequently registered 40 degrees below zero.

Of the 38 stranded men, 8 were sourdoughs who, under adverse conditions, guided the unskilled in improvising shelter. Mattresses and blankets had been salvaged for all, but few were fortunate enough to have warm clothing. Stoves were fashioned from pieces of metal so each rough shelter had one, but the chill was so penetrating that it was difficult to keep from freezing. Men were frostbitten while they slept. They lived on mulligan stew, mush, a few flapjacks and pork chops. Blizzards raged and longing for a rescue ship mounted to a frenzy. As the month of February began, some items of food ran short. The *Farallon,* still on the rock, was covered with ice. Every rope had a great white frozen cannonball hanging from it.

Soon after the wreck Captain Hunter asked the mate, Gus Swanson, and five volunteers to go to Cape Douglas 40 miles away and build a large fire to attract attention, or continue to Kodiak if possible. As the weeks went by nothing was heard from them and no vessel arrived.

Meanwhile, at the end of January, when it was presumed some accident had befallen the ship, the *Dora* set out in search of her. It was Feb. 4 before the *Victoria,* cruising in the same waters, sighted the wreck. The ice on the *Farallon* caused her to blend with the snowy landscape, and the camp was hidden behind her on the dazzling white beach. The *Victoria* would have missed the stranded vessel, had not a fireman with field glasses spotted a small boat coming out from shore with several men.

The *Victoria* was obliged to stand off a mile and a half from land. It required a day and a half to bring aboard the survivors through the slushy ice to the steamer, which was in danger of freezing in. The men had to climb a rope ladder up the sides. The sea was so rough that the cook, who was beginning to feel sick, could not manage the ascent and had to be brought up in a net sling.

The search was not over, for the revenue cutter *Tahoma* was seeking the six men who had left for Cape Douglas. They had reached the cape during a storm and attempted to land. Their lifeboat was wrecked; they were thrown into the sea, provisions and bedding lost. Their clothing froze. The engineer, Al Bailey, cut switches and beat the men, which angered them, roused them and set them moving. Several days later they found a Native woman with a cache of skins. She gave them some food, mostly whale blubber, and told them how to find the nearest Indian village. They remained a month with a trapper there, then mushed through the snow to the next community 80 miles away. There they obtained a dory, and went along the coast to a bay where they found a sturdier boat, and crossed Shelikof Strait to Miners Point on Kodiak Island. Once more they were wrecked in attempting to land. They reached the beach, mushed over mountains to Uganik, then went by dory to Afognak. Here they were discovered by the crew of the *Tahoma* on March 7, picked up and taken home.

The survivors of the *Farallon* were not yet back in civilization when word was received that another company ship, the *Yucatan,* had struck an iceberg in Icy Strait and stove a hole in her bow. The

**Securing provisions from the wreck of the
SS _Farallon_ in Iliamna Bay.**
Puget Sound Maritime Historical Society

Survivors of the *Farallon* wreck. There were few provisions for winter survival.
Puget Sound Maritime Historical Society

accident occurred after dark during a snowstorm. No jar was felt when she struck. The first intimation of disaster was when several sailors sacking coal noticed that water was coming into the hold. Capt. W.P.S. Porter headed for the beach immediately and sent the first mate with five seamen in a small boat for help. Provisions and bedding were taken in lifeboats and landed on Goose Island, where canvas lean-tos were erected. The first mate and his crew rowed fifteen miles before they met a launch which took them to Juneau. Here they obtained help from the *Georgia* which was immediately dispatched to bring in the seventy passengers, who by this time had reached Hoonah.

The *Yucatan* lay on even keel, partly submerged at low tide. She was abandoned to the underwriters, refloated in May, and towed to Portland for repairs. After being in the coastal service a while she was sold to Japanese interests.

Loss of the *Olympia* ended the year's disasters. She had discharged most of her cargo in Cordova. Nearly all the remainder, intended for Valdez, was stowed forward, which made her bow-heavy and compounded steering difficulties. A heavy snowstorm, driven by a 50-mile gale, overtook her in Prince William Sound. Capt. Jim Daniels attempted to steer clear of Bligh Island, but the gale had fixed the ship's course and she could not respond. At 12:20 a.m., Dec. 11, 1910, she struck a submerged reef.

It was soon ascertained that she was in a firm position, which was fortunate as lifeboats would have had trouble in the

The SS *Farallon* with a sheathing of ice. ▶
Puget Sound Maritime Historical Society

SS *Alameda*
Joe D. Williamson

wind and high seas. As the fires went out on the *Olympia,* all aboard suffered from the intense cold while they waited for assistance to come. The ship's radioman had kept busy sending distress signals until the power went off, but there were no boats closer than Katalla to go to her aid. It was not until the *Dora* was reached by radio at Seward that help was sent. A government boat, the *Donaldson,* also came out. The crew managed to serve meals during the long wait, until 4:30 in the afternoon when the *Donaldson* hove in sight.

The *Olympia*'s bottom was badly torn and salvage was never attempted. She sat on the rocks on a nearly even keel until February 1922 — a landmark for local sailors. From a distance she looked as though she were afloat.

Captain Daniels' one-year suspension after the wreck was reduced to two months because the lack of navigation aids and the storm had contributed to the disaster.

Development of wireless communications made a great difference in the lonely reaches of the North. Survivors were never again subjected to such long waits as those of the *Farallon.* Several years after radio was first installed, the Marconi Wireless Telegraph Company absorbed the earlier United Wireless Telegraph Company and immediately raised the cost of service to a prohibitive figure. A Seattle firm, Kilbourne and Clark, offered a better price for radio service, which Alaska Steam accepted. Marconi sued for infringement of its patent, but lost the case.

With the advent of radio telegraph, C.B. Cooper became superintendent of radio service for the fleet. Later Kilbourne and Clark took him into their organization. An arrangement was made to service each ship at so much a month, with the firm furnishing operators.

Radio was not yet sufficiently developed to supply entertainment for passengers as well as message service. The installation in 1912 of Victrolas in mahogany cases on the *Mariposa, Alameda, Northwestern, Victoria, Dolphin* and *Jefferson* was the last word in shipboard entertainment in those days.

Next acquisition was the *Alameda,* purchased in 1910 from Oceanic Steamship Co., and put on the southwestern Alaska run. She was destined to be in the firm's service a long time. She was an old boat, built in 1883, and operated to Hawaii and Australia. When Alaska Steam acquired the *Alameda* she was fitted to accommodate 202 first-class passengers and 400 steerage; the dining room could seat 96 at a time and the social hall was advertised as "sumptuously furnished."

The *Alameda* had not flown the company flag long when she met with an accident. On Dec. 10, 1910, she left Cordova empty after unloading coal, her bow high out of the water. She was headed for Valdez when a storm arose, causing her to steer so badly that she, too, was stranded on Bligh Island. There was no opportunity to put out lifeboats, so the fearful passengers spent the night aboard, buffeted by a gale. They got off the next day with no loss of life.

Delivery of coal to Cordova figured in another episode of that period, likened at the time to the Boston tea party.

Alaskans had a chronic allergy to monopolies. In the old days large companies had dominated whaling and the

The dining salon aboard the SS *Alameda.*
Puget Sound Maritime Historical Society

The winter scene at Cordova's ocean dock.

capture of fur seals, and after them came the chains of trading company stores. Now the Morgan-Guggenheim syndicate controlled a railroad, a steamboat line, canneries and mines. Many people were suspicious of these developments and feared that the Territory's resources and politics would fall into the hands of the syndicate.

It is true that when the company was launching the mines at Kennecott, it considered erecting a smelter at Mile 40 on the railroad and constructing a branch line to the Controller Bay coalfields. Surveys were completed and work was about to begin, when suddenly the U.S. government passed a law withdrawing all coal and oil lands in Alaska from entry. Plans for the rail extension were abandoned. Proceedings were initiated to cancel existing rights, but the men who had staked 37 coal claims in the vicinity of Katalla clung to them stubbornly.

Simon Guggenheim defended the syndicate's right to develop the coal at the 1910 meeting of the American Mining Congress, saying that the natural resources of the area belonged to the people, but were quite valueless until discovered, developed, linked with the world and made productive and profitable. This development called for men, capital and risks.

A strong faction in Alaska resented the interference of Pres. Theodore Roosevelt and his Secretary of the Interior, Gifford Pinchot, in the development of such resources as the coalfields. Cordova residents, in particular, could not see why they should pay a high price for coal from British Columbia when exploitation of the neighboring coal beds was banned. This vexation came to a head on May 3, 1911, with a "coal party," inspiring a headline in a Seattle paper: ALASKA BEGINS BLOODLESS REVOLT. The story told how several hundred citizens marched to Cordova's ocean dock and shoveled a pile of 100 tons of Canadian coal into the harbor as a protest. Telegrams had been sent to Washington asking the government to reopen the Bering River and Katalla coalfields. When no replies were received, the people took matters into their own hands.

Richard J. Barry, agent for the Alaska Steamship Co., cabled Mayor Austin D. Lathrop of Cordova and demanded that the coal on the dock, which was company property, be protected, only to be told the deputy U.S. marshal was out of town and the U.S. commissioner could not be found.

Chief of Police Dooley appeared at the dock flourishing a gun, but the crowd greeted him with cries of, "Give us Alaska coal." Agent Barry was armed also, but he and the policeman could do nothing in the face of the mob. When workmen arrived from the railroad shops to back up Dooley, the president of the Chamber of Commerce shouted, "Shovel away, boys."

The pile was large and cooler heads eventually prevailed upon the shovelers to taper off their effort and disperse, because the company and not the government would suffer the loss. Mayor Lathrop wired President Taft that the situation was desperate. While excitement mounted in Cordova, Katalla citizens were burning Pinchot in effigy.

Another steamship, the *Edith*, was due to arrive shortly with 2,000 more tons of Nanaimo coal. The townspeople were talking of using explosives to get rid of it.

The minute the freighter came within the three-mile limit, it was predicted launches would come out to meet her. The *Northwestern* was also scheduled to arrive from Seattle, but Alaska Line officials declared that she carried only American coal. The agent beseeched the citizens to make no demonstration aboard her. A rope was stretched across the dock and deputy marshals prevented citizens from approaching the vessel. In the meantime the remainder of the offending coal had been sacked and sent inland.

Still the *Edith* came on. It was rumored she might take her coal to Seward. The next report was that agent Barry was trying to get a government vessel, the *Buffalo*, normally engaged in repairing wireless stations, to convoy the freighter into port.

Much sympathy was expressed for the rioters and, although warrants were issued for arrest of their leaders, it was felt strongly that they would not be prosecuted. In an interview, even the head of the Alaska Line said he understood the aims of the local citizens. The *Seattle Times* observed, "These people of the North, bands of determined men who have endured every hardship and suffered every vicissitude and privation, at last have determined to take the law into their own hands and by force take possession of the properties which they discovered and to reap some of the fruits of their toil."

Isaac Guggenheim, hearing in New York of the Cordova coal party, staunchly denied that his company owned one foot of coal land in Alaska, and said the government would not permit anyone to touch it.

By the time the *Edith* finally hove in sight on May 11, the ardor of the rioters had cooled. A railroad crew had worked all night clearing away rocks dumped on the tracks to prevent trains from reaching her coal. Deputy marshals were out in force to control the crowd gathered again on the dock. But the ship unloaded without trouble and no prosecution ever followed the coal party. A year later, under Wickersham's Home Rule bill, the coal lands that had been closed since 1906 were reopened.

CHAPTER 4

Expansion and Change

The Alaska Steamship Company seemed to specialize in second-hand vessels, refurbishing them to its own requirements. In three-quarters of a century of operation only four ships were built to order for the company: the *Jefferson, Latouche, Kennecott* and the second *Alaska.* The *Alameda, Mariposa* and the first *Alaska* were altered very little when added to the fleet. The most visible change, on all three vessels, was the addition of an observation room on the boat deck aft. This extended the public space and provided a sheltered vantage point during inclement weather.

The most durable of all the company ships was the *Victoria.* She became a legend in the Bering Sea, for she led the traffic into Nome each spring when the ice broke up. A former resident of that city wrote of the grand old lady of the fleet, "Her deep-throated whistle in the roadstead after the spring breakup brought all Nome down to the beach. Some cried,

◀SS *Victoria* in a Bremerton, Washington, dry dock.

some laughed, some stood tight and tense. She brought Christmas packages and other mail that piled up beyond the 2,000 pounds dog teams were allowed to carry. She brought head lettuce! And women passengers dressed in the latest styles, which often caused eyes to bug.''

Capt. Maurice Reaber said the residents of Nome placed so much trust in the *Victoria* that when the Alaska Line proposed putting another ship on the run, a petition was circulated asking that it not be done.

The *Victoria* was famed for her gold cargoes. Trip after trip she carried up to $2 million out of Nome. The bricks were shipped in canvas bags valued at $20,000 each. Often there was not sufficient room for them in the safe so they were stacked on the floor of the purser's office. At times in late fall the ship waited as long as two weeks in Nome to give miners a chance for a final cleanup before she came out.

Captain Reaber said one mining company used heavy iron-locked containers for shipping its gold bullion. He noted one incident when, at the end of a trip, a container rolled out of the sling at Pier 2, and its door flew open. It had been in the 'tween decks with the door unlocked for the entire voyage. There were a few exciting moments when people on deck were forced to stand back, expecting gold to cascade down around them. Nothing spilled from the bags — the gold landed safely.

At one time the *Victoria* carried two gamblers known familiarly as Spaghetti Dan and Ryan. "They ran a game down below," Reaber related, "relieving the prospectors of their hard-earned money. The gamblers went along every trip, as regularly as members of the crew. The only time I saw the bank busted was on one return trip, when we stopped at False Pass to pick up salmon and the Chinese cannery crew. Soon a big game was under way and in a few days the Chinese cleaned Dan and Ryan out. What broke them was that every time a Chinese won a pot, he took it down and hid it in his mattress. Money was leaving the game all the time.

"Gambling was stopped in later years, but if you looked around you'd find there was always gambling going on. Then there was the pool on each day's run; passengers put a lot of money on it."

Reaber described the perennial stowaway who was aboard the first trip every season. "He was a fellow who worked for the Nome lighterage company," Reaber said, "and stowing away was something he wanted to prove he could do. We always knew he was aboard, and we had to find him or he would starve. Usually he would turn up the first day or two, but one time it must have taken five days, until a crew member went into No. 2 hold where a little noise had been heard coming from a bunch of shingles. We pulled them apart and found our man. He had built himself a little house under the shingles, but his food was gone. We dragged him to the purser's office, signed him on for his passage, and put him in the room which his company was paying for."

Stories about the *Victoria* are almost endless. One summer a competing ship, the *Buford,* was on the run to Nome with the *Victoria,* and the two entered port neck and neck. To beat the San Francisco boat, the *Vic* went inside the reef at Cape Mohican on Nunivak Island and followed along the Yukon flats, making up enough time to arrive first. There was a full load of passengers, and betting was heavy on which craft would get in first.

The *Victoria* carried many famous persons to the North, among them Roald Amundsen, the arctic explorer, who used to go up on the bridge and check out the instruments he was going to use on his own ship, the *Maud.*

The *Victoria* was one of the first vessels on the Pacific Coast to be equipped with wireless. On her way out in 1912, she was able to flash word of the Mount Katmai eruption. The *Dora* was proceeding northeast up Shelikof Strait at the time, and some aboard her got pictures of the eruption. On many winter voyages the two ships had been ice-covered, but this was their only experience with a coating furnished by a volcano. Ash five to six inches deep covered the *Dora,* and the mail clerk, an aggressive free-lance newspaper correspondent, made photographs of it to accompany his story. He also showed the heavy cloud of smoke rising from the peak.

The blanket of volcanic dust traveled faster than the vessel and in a few hours overtook it and hid the entrance to Kodiak harbor, so the *Dora* was obliged to forego her usual call. She traveled through a day of darkness punctuated by bursts of lightning and the din of heavy thunder. Birds overcome by the sulfurous fumes fell onto the deck. The ship became exceedingly hot from the heat of the ash. which permeated her throughout, even the engine room.

Few Alaskans knew exactly where the eruption had occurred, and the *Dora's* men were the first to report the source of the ash. They took a bearing on Katmai immediately upon seeing the black cloud mushrooming from the peak. Part of the mountaintop appeared to have blown off.

Almost as fondly regarded as the *Victoria* in those early decades of the century was the *Alameda.* In the spring of 1912 the company, having observed how successful she was in the Alaskan trade, purchased her sister ship, the *Mariposa,* from the Oceanic Steamship Company. She was another iron-hulled vessel, built in 1883, of 3,158 tons registry. These two steamships were faster than previous craft and cut the time from Seattle to Ketchikan from 52 hours to a little more than 41 hours.

In July 1912 the company bought the freighter *Cordova* while she was under construction at Wilmington, Delaware. She had been designed as a lumber carrier of 2,273 tons, but the company had other uses in mind for her. The *Cordova* was an oil-burner and in that year few ports existed where fuel could be replenished for the voyage around Cape Horn to the Pacific Coast. The last place on the East Coast where she could fill up was Jacksonville, Florida. The ship had to make it around to Taltal, Chile, before she

Volcanic ash at Kodiak, June 1912.

SS Mariposa
Joe D. Williamson

could obtain more oil. She had only 90 barrels left when she arrived there.

One of the *Cordova*'s mishaps occurred when she ran aground in January 1913 in Wrangell Narrows. The crew had to pump 50 barrels of crude oil into the channel to lighten and refloat her, but she was not badly damaged.

The *Cordova*, under command of Capt. Thomas Moore, was at Nome on Sept. 20, 1914, when word was received of the wreck of the revenue cutter *Tahoma* on a jagged reef in the western Aleutians. By the time the *Cordova* reached Unimak Pass she was informed by the Unalga radio station that no ships had gone to the rescue. It was up to Captain Moore to make an effort to save the officers and crew. He set course for Kiska, arriving there on Sept. 25 and, after cruising a day and a night, sighted a light bobbing up and down on the swells. It proved to be one of the *Tahoma*'s boats with the master, Capt. Richard O. Crisp, and ten of the crew. They had been out five days, were soaking wet, and had used up most of their provisions. They described the rapid sinking of the revenue cutter and said they had barely got away.

The search for more survivors continued and a few hours later another boat with 11 men was sighted near Agattu Island. At 3 p.m., a third boat was found with 14 men. Then the *Cordova* steered toward the Semichi Islands, and on the evening of the 26th found a fourth lifeboat with 26 persons. Others were still missing. Sailors were sent ashore at Attu to seek survivors, but found none. After that, the *Cordova* communicated by radio with the Coast and Geodetic Survey ship *Patterson,* which had arrived in the vicinity. On the evening of the 28th, the survey ship announced that she had found 29 more men, the remainder of the cutter's crew.

The *Cordova* had been out 36 days and had consumed most of her oil. Captain Moore set a course for Akutan, and arrived there on Oct. 14 with his tanks almost empty. He obtained a refill at the whaling station, then went on to Latouche to load copper ore, and then to Kasaan and Santa Ana in southeastern Alaska to take on canned salmon. The *Cordova* arrived in Seattle Oct. 21 with 3,000 tons of cargo, after a record voyage of 59 days, covering 7,902 miles.

During 1912 and 1913 there were important changes for the administration of the company and also in the Territory. In August 1912 Alaska gained a legislature of its own. At Alaska Steam, Joseph Young, who had succeeded Peabody, retired from the presidency at the end of 1912 and was replaced by S.W. Eccles. Robert W. Baxter resigned from the Union Pacific Railroad to become vice-president in charge, in Seattle, of both the steamship company and the Copper River and Northwestern Railroad.

Excursions to Alaska were increasing in popularity, and in its advertising literature the company called attention to opportunities to view the glaciers. Passengers making the $100 round-trip to Seward and back to Seattle were treated to a railroad jaunt out of Cordova. On the way north they stopped at Ketchikan, Juneau, Skagway (on some runs), Valdez and Latouche, where they were urged to buy baskets and other souvenirs brought to the docks by Indian vendors. The *Alameda, Mariposa* and *Northwestern* served this route while the *Dolphin* and *Jefferson* were on the Sitka run.

Because confusion in departure times had led to many misunderstandings, an announcement was made that, "Hereafter all notices of sailing time shall be in the time of the port where the vessel is." This change in procedure pleased Alaska residents.

In 1915 more vessels were added to the fleet. The *Dirigo* had been lost the previous November, so the company purchased the *Kansas City* from the Portland and San Francisco Steamship Company, remodeled her, and named her the *Alaska*. She was built in 1889 for the New England and Savannah Steamship Company, a fashionable carrier between New York and Savannah. She went on the run to Seward and, in March 1917, set a record by covering the 754 miles from Ketchikan to Seattle in 40 hours.

The company also acquired the *Redondo*, a tubby 695-ton freighter built in 1902. She was sent to westward ports and was useful around canneries.

Folders issued for the 1915 season announced that for the first time the *Mariposa* and *Northwestern* would go to Cook Inlet to a new dot on the map known as Knik Anchorage. Travelers were counseled to make reservations early because much business was expected that year for two reasons: the San Francisco World's Fair would bring many Easterners to the Pacific Coast, and it was likely a certain percentage would be interested in seeing Alaska.

The other incentive to travel was construction of another railroad to the Interior. For a number of years it had been rumored that a rail line eventually would be built out of Seward. Surveys began in 1903 and a group of Seattle capitalists organized the Alaska Central Railroad.

The former Kansas City, renamed Alaska.
Joe D. Williamson

Construction on the old gold-seekers trail that would become the Richardson Highway to Fairbanks.

Construction started the following year, but in 1908 the line went into receivership. In April 1912, the project was taken over by the Alaska Northwestern Railroad and the single track was extended to Turnagain Arm. The total length was still little more than 70 miles.

Because it was apparent something had to be done to promote development of the natural resources of the Territory of Alaska, a commission was appointed to organize a government-built-and-operated line. A route was surveyed up the shore of Turnagain Arm to the Susitna Valley and Nenana, and in 1915 the government purchased the existing railroad out of Seward. A construction base was established where Ship Creek enters Knik Arm, equipment and materials were landed, and a town of 2,000 sprang up. Anchorage was born.

The wharf at Seward was repaired and the Alaska Northern line was rehabilitated. The first winter shipments went in by way of Seward and were carried from the end of rails by dog team. In 1916 the Admiral Line (which was the advertising slogan for the Pacific Steamship Company) had sailings up Cook Inlet to Anchorage. So did the government transport *Crook*, which was assigned to carry workers and supplies for the railroad job all that summer.

As the United States became involved in the war in Europe, construction costs increased and labor became difficult to obtain. Many men who might have remained in Alaska enlisted in the Canadian army or returned to the United States to work in war industries. Nonetheless, though plagued by shortages of materials, the railroad slowly crept toward its goal.

Naturally the Alaska Steamship Company secured some of the business in the Cook Inlet region, although that waterway was noted for its excessively high tides and great run-outs. It had been served in the past by shallow-draft vessels. The *Mariposa* went all the way to Anchorage in the wintry month of November 1917, carrying an Army detachment of 40 men for the barracks. The *Alameda* also made calls at the new port.

In addition to the Alaska Railroad, another large construction project was under way during this period. The Richardson Highway was being built from Valdez to Fairbanks. First the old government trail was improved for winter travel by horse-drawn sleds; then it was widened and graded for stages and wagons. In 1913 the first automobile crossed over it. Eventually it became part of a loop route for touring parties.

The four active ports of Seward, Valdez, Latouche and Cordova on Prince William Sound served the increasing marine traffic. This increase sparked the building of another lighthouse, completed in September 1916, at Cape St. Elias. Copper continued to be the staple outbound cargo from this region the year around. After vessels unloaded passengers and cargo at Seattle they regularly went to the Tacoma smelter dock to give up their copper. Any gold ore brought south was unloaded onto flatcars at Seattle and sent to Kellogg, Idaho.

The mines had commenced shipping concentrates instead of crude ore from Latouche in 1915. The ore at Latouche was very low grade. The method of concentration was a patented process using what was known as Barrett oil. The powdered ore was floated down a small flume containing water and a pine oil

The SS *Edith* foundering off Alaska's coast.

solution. A paddle-like device kept the mixture agitated, creating large bubbles. The copper clung to the bubbles, then was scraped off and carried to a dryer. From there the concentrate was stored in large bins on the dock for transfer in bulk to the hold of a ship. The product to be shipped was a wet, oily, slippery mass, somewhat like mud. In spite of an effort to dry the concentrates, they were extremely difficult to ship.

The freighter *Seward* was the first to experience trouble, with a 3,800-ton ore cargo that shifted at sea. She was obliged to head for Cordova, where she lay at the wharf listing so badly that her rail was under the water. She narrowly escaped "turning turtle" and it was thought she would have to be beached. The trouble was rectified in time, but it was only a month later when disaster caught up to another ore carrier, the *Edith*. She was another of the company's old British-built iron boats, dating from 1882, formerly the *Glenochil* of the Glen line. She, too, had been a troop transport in the Spanish American War. When it came to transporting ore the *Edith* had always been a cranky ship, and on several occasions she had to return to port to have her cargo restowed so she would not list heavily.

On Aug. 29, 1915, heavily laden with ore, the *Edith* sailed out of Latouche. When the *Mariposa* passed her in Prince William Sound early the next morning, she was on even keel. Outside of Cape Hinchinbrook a heavy sea was running. The steamer got into trouble immediately. As she rolled, the moist concentrates shifted, putting her on beam end. Fearing that she was about to sink, Capt. C.B. McMullen ordered the crew into lifeboats. A distress call was sent out and the *Mariposa* hurried to her aid, reached her at 9 p.m., and took her in tow. By eight o'clock the next morning, 46 miles off Cape St. Elias, she had to be abandoned. Lights were hung up on the derelict hull and she appeared to be sinking. Eventually she drifted ashore near the cape and broke up. All of the crew were saved, but $150,000 worth of copper was lost. The *Edith* had been the second-largest freighter on the northern routes, exceeded in size only by the *Seward.*

After the sinking of the *Edith,* the process of preparing copper concentrates was improved so they were drier. To make their shipment even safer, large bins were constructed in the holds to keep the copper concentrate from shifting. Ore from the Kennecott mine was placed in heavy jute sacks; each sack held about 200 pounds. It took two men with cargo hooks to load each full sack. The sacks were returned from the smelter after being laundered and patched.

"The sacks were often frozen," explained Frank Burns, former company agent at Cordova. "They were dumped on the dock and were hard to pull apart, so a big hoist picked them off. Snow interrupted railroad service in winter, so the company stockpiled ore out of McCarthy. Milling went on for most of the winter and high-grade ore piled up at the mine. The ore was left in dump cars along the tracks in Cordova and piled all over the railroad yards. Some of it was dumped off beside the tracks."

In April 1915, the Kennecott Copper Company was formed and began acquiring stock in the Alaska Steamship Company, which was then operating 10 vessels, a total of 31,854 gross tons. At the close of the year the copper company owned 43 percent of the stock. By the end of 1925 it possessed 100 percent.

The biggest year for the corporation's mines was 1916. Metals were in demand because of World War I; 120 million pounds of copper went out on company ships. During that year the *Seward* was chartered to Frank Waterhouse and Company to carry railroad equipment and war munitions to Vladivostok. That ship had large hatches suitable for handling entire flatcars, so she brought a charter price of $1,000 a day; a record then for vessels of this class. On her return from the Siberian coast she was chartered to Proctor and Gamble for $40,000 a month to carry olive oil and other soap-making materials. Proctor and Gamble bought her in June 1916. The *Seward* had a short life after that; during the war she was sunk by torpedoes off the coast of France.

Alaska Steam needed more freighters, so in June 1916 the company purchased the *Bennington*, 2,382 tons, and the *Burlington*, 2,308 tons, and rechristened them the *Valdez* and *Juneau*. Both had been built in 1908 for the Rutland Transit Company. In July 1916, the *Eureka*, 2,373 tons, was acquired from the Pacific Coast Steamship Company and renamed *Ketchikan.* Later her name was changed again to *Nizina.*

Another purchase during World War I was the *Stanley Dollar* in 1917 from the Dollar Steamship Company. She was renamed the *Skagway*. In August 1916, the line bought the *Henry T. Scott* and chartered that freighter to a towing service carrying nitrates from Antofagasta, Chile, to the Panama Canal. During the war the passenger ships

The SS *Mariposa* after she had been beached.
Joe D. Williamson

Alameda, Alaska, Jefferson, Mariposa, Northwestern and *Victoria* remained on their customary routes. The *Dolphin* was sold in South America. In the summer of 1916, the company scheduled 11 sailings a month. It offered two exceptional tours of nearly the entire Alaskan coastline aboard the *Victoria.* The ship first went directly to Nome, then returned south by way of the southwestern and southeastern ports, and included visits to Columbia and Miles glaciers. It was considered a special event when a captain would blow his whistle and cause chunks to fall off the great body of ice and float away.

Late in 1917, calamity befell the *Mariposa.* She had come down from Anchorage and gone into Shakan to load salmon at the cannery. It was a difficult place to get in and out of. The *Mariposa* left Shakan at 3 a.m. on Nov. 18, and less than two hours later crashed into the rocks head-on, damaging her plates forward. Soon she was leaking, then her oil tanks burst. According to a story that came out later, the young pilot on duty at the time had become confused about the location of the light and he went to Capt. Charles O'Brien for advice. The skipper had just retired and was in an ill-tempered mood, and so he sent the pilot back to the bridge. The young fellow, instead of stopping the ship, held his course and crashed. The *Mariposa* listed so sharply to starb'rd that it was apparent she might slip off the reef and turn over. Captain O'Brien came rushing out and ordered her abandoned. He and five of the crew remained with the *Mariposa* until she began to slip off the reef. By 9:38 a.m. she was gone, carrying nearly 25,000 cases of salmon and 1,200 tons of copper ore with her. The 265 passengers on board were taken off without mishap and later picked up by the *Curacao, Ravalli* and *Jefferson,* which brought most of them to Seattle. On board the *Mariposa* were the crews of two other wrecked vessels, who had had their fill of misadventure by the time they reached home.

Adventure still lived in the North. An excursion folder suggested that passengers from Outside would have a great opportunity to mix with Alaska residents on board and surely could "get much more out of the trip on this account." A traveler on Alaska Steam might talk with Kodiak bear hunters from New York, schoolteachers who had dreamed of an Alaskan cruise for years, miners from Kennecott, millers from Latouche, fur trappers from Gulkana, fishermen from Bristol Bay and missionaries from the Aleutian Islands.

Year after year each passenger list contained a *Who's Who* of territorial luminaries, plus an assortment of homebodies traveling because of family or business obligations. "Riding the Alaska Line was like being in a good hotel," an Anchorage resident recalled recently. "The ships provided tasty food, sociability — all one could ask for."

Elizabeth S. Hakkinen, now curator of the Sheldon Museum in Haines, recalls, "My father, Steve Sheldon, made his first trip to Alaska as storekeeper on the *Northwestern* in June 1908. My own first-ever trip Outside was on the *Northwestern* in 1930. On the voyages, when we would stop at canneries, several of us would get a sack lunch from the galley and hike all over the hills in the vicinity. College students southbound would board at each southeast Alaska town and we were pretty well acquainted by the time we reached Seattle. We could come home COD in the spring, frequently catching the same ship."

The mingling of people from the Territory on the Alaska Line played a part in romance and political maneuvers. The ships brought together residents from scattered districts and gave them an opportunity to get acquainted.

Robert C. Rose, former general passenger agent, observed, "Until the second World War there wasn't any way to get to Alaska except by ship. People from Ketchikan, Juneau and Anchorage, aboard for several days, got to know residents of other regions. They danced, played cards, had a drink and dined with those from distant sections of Alaska. A great many families are the result of a shipboard romance, when boy met girl on the *Northwestern* or the *Victoria*. We received many letters from couples asking for pictures of the ship where they had originally met."

News in Alaskan ports centered to a large extent upon the arrival and departure of the steamers. Boat day was a busy one for local reporters. Besides the information residents brought back from the States, usually several famous persons aboard were worthy of interviews. No matter what hour the vessel docked, some editorial representative was on hand to scan the passenger list and track down celebrities. This was the most exciting part of the townsfolks' week, for not only passengers arrived, but letters, parcels, newspapers and fresh produce for the stores. For several hours the main street would be alive with groups of visitors and with local shoppers eager to purchase fruits and vegetables.

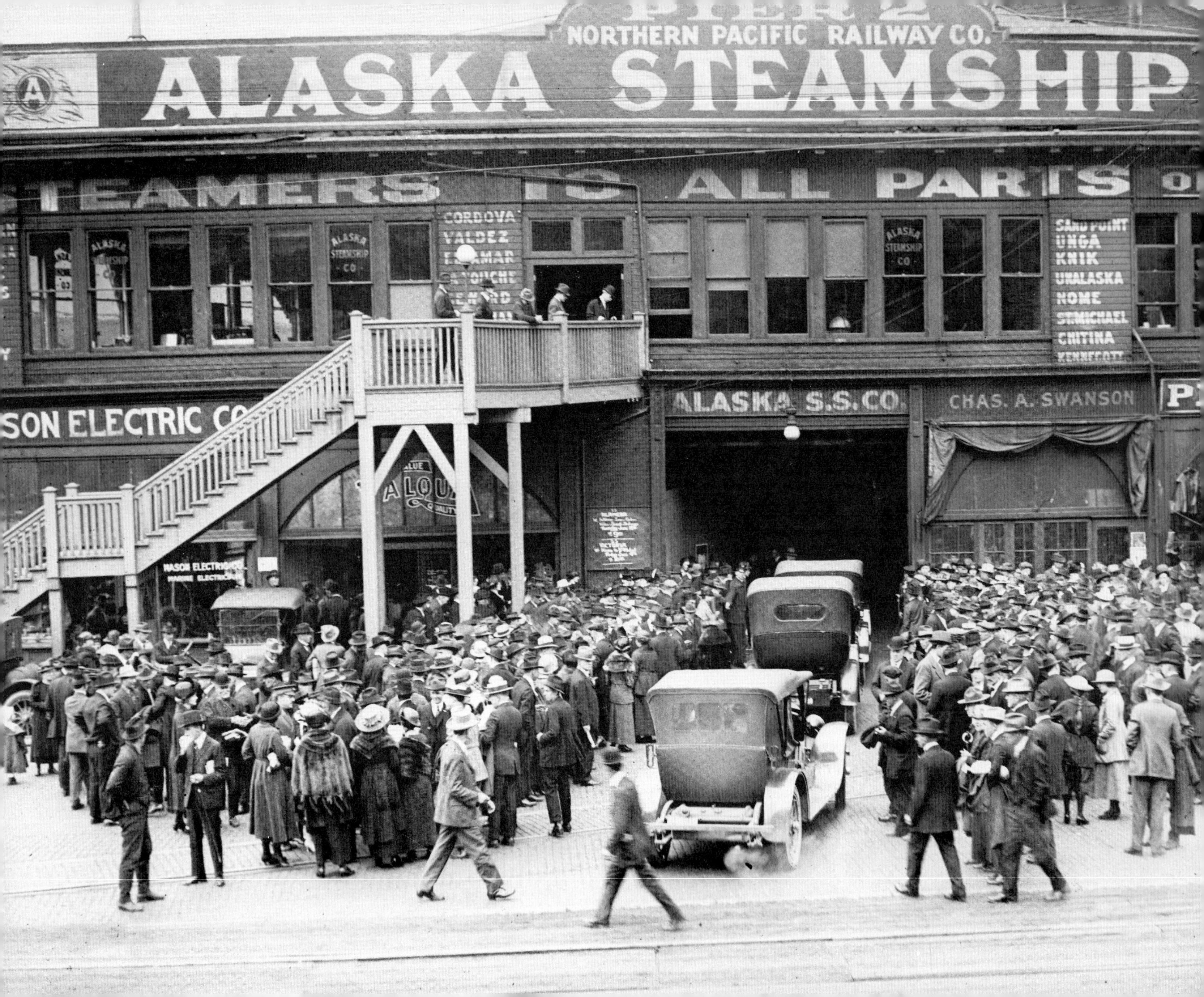
NORTHERN PACIFIC RAILWAY CO.
ALASKA STEAMSHIP
ALL PARTS
CORDOVA
VALDEZ
ALASKA STEAMSHIP CO
SAND POINT
UNGA
KNIK
UNALASKA
NOME
ST MICHAEL
CHITINA
KENNECOTT
ALASKA S.S. CO.
CHAS. A. SWANSON

CHAPTER 5

Passenger Traffic and Prohibition

As the first World War drew toward its end, Alaska Steam had to cope with increased operational costs. The company, therefore, requested the U.S. Shipping Board to permit rate increases for the 1918 and 1919 seasons. Hearings were held in both Seattle and the Alaskan ports, where residents of the North protested that any raises would inflict a hardship. The company outlined a number of reasons why the old rates were insufficient. Additional revenue was needed to replace ships lost at sea and obsolete ships, and to pay the increased costs of operation. Representatives of the firm also described the uncertainties of doing business in Alaska, the uncharted coast along which the ships sailed, the high tides, bad weather, seasonality of commerce and poor dock facilities. After considering these factors the Shipping Board found higher charges reasonable.

Pier 2, Seattle, was embarkation point for Alaska for decades. A sailing for the North was well attended as this early '20s crowd suggests.
Joe D. Williamson

In 1918 Stephen Birch, the man who launched the Kennecott mine, became president of both the steamship and railroad companies, succeeding S.W. Eccles, who had died in New York.

Business went along as usual that season; the customary quota of minor accidents was recorded. Early in the year a rumor reached Juneau that the *Alaska* had struck an iceberg and gone down with great loss of life. There was rejoicing when it was learned that she was in Cordova and all right. On July 17 the *Alameda* hit rocks at Sawmill Bay, outside of Latouche, and developed a 15-degree list. After three hours she was assisted off her perch by a number of small motorboats from nearby villages, and was able to proceed in spite of some damage.

Just below Swanson's Bay, British Columbia, in the early-morning darkness and mist of Oct. 20, the *Alaska* had the misfortune to strike rocks, breaking her steering gear. She put her passengers ashore. A Canadian coaster, the *Chelohsin*, picked up the distress call, then took the stranded travelers to the little town nearby. The northbound

Jefferson came to the ship's aid, turned about, and with the *Alaska*'s passengers on board, accompanied her to Seattle, where she delivered her load of copper safely.

October saw the end of the line's ownership of the venerable *Dora.* This old workhorse was sold to Bering Sea Fisheries.

For the Alaska Steamship Company, the only newsworthy event in 1919 occurred when the *Northwestern* grounded on Anchor Point in Wrangell Narrows and had to be pulled off. She was unhurt.

In 1920 Congress passed the Jones Merchant Marine Act, which greatly affected the company's future and the Territory as a whole. The purpose of the measure was to promote American shipping; it stressed the importance of keeping American coastwise trading in American-built ships. No merchandise was to be transported between ports in the United States, either directly or by way of a foreign port, in any but American vessels. This law prevented competition from Canadian shipping and excluded any possibility of routing goods through British Columbia. Some Alaskans bitterly opposed the act, and made an attempt to have the Supreme Court declare it unconstitutional. The attempt was unsuccessful, and the Jones Act remains in effect to this day.

E.T. Stannard, superintendent of the Kennecott mine, was put in charge of Alaska Steam's Seattle operations in 1920. Soon afterward the company began doing its own repair work except for drydocking, having leased a special building and lay-up wharf in West Seattle for the purpose. Deck officers and others were

Front

▲
Promotional materials touting travel to Alaska.

ALASKA
is calling
YOU!

Visit the land of the Midnight Sun, dazzling Glaciers, inspiring Fjords and weird Totems.

See the Gold and Copper Mines, Fisheries and Salmon Canneries in operation.

Sail Alaska's azure waters, flanked by evergreen shores and towering snowcapped mountains.

Tour our Northern Wonderland while it is still primeval.

Alaska is calling **NOW — Lets Go!**

If you have already planned your vacation this year—start now planning **YOUR ALASKA TRIP** for next year.

Remember it may be cheaper to **VACATION IN ALASKA** than to stay at home. Write for all the information and maps. Fares include berth and meals. You'll be surprised how reasonable, too.

Address
L. W. BAKER,
General Freight and Passenger Agent,
ALASKA STEAMSHIP COMPANY
Pier 2 -   -   Seattle
or

WHEN YOU THINK ALASKA—THINK ALASKA STEAMSHIP COMPANY

Back

A display promoting the Golden Belt Line Tours to Alaska. The exhibit designer made ▶ extensive decorative use of the "totem" shown above.

ALASKA STEAMSHIP COMPANY

To Really See Alaska—
—make The GOLDEN BELT LINE TOUR

given the opportunity to do repair work during the off-season, the winter months.

The Volstead Act of 1920 prohibited the sale and consumption of liquor in the United States and its territories. This act, unpopular and unenforceable, was repealed in 1935. The interval between those years, known simply as "during Prohibition," was a time when a great many otherwise law-abiding citizens found ingenious ways to produce or obtain liquor, for their own consumption or for sale at exhorbitant profit.

Alaska was and still is hard-liquor country, and no matter what efforts Alaska Steam made to conform with the law, drinking was bound to go on aboard the ships. In August 1920, it was rumored that Scotch whisky was retailed at $25 a quart to passengers on the *Victoria*'s first trip of the season to Nome. It was said that the ship hove to somewhere en route, and took aboard a slingload of beer and whiskey from a small craft — presumably Canadian, as Canada was known to be amused by, and to profit from, its neighbor's experiment in abstinence by legislation. Whatever the truth of this story, the captain was quietly relieved of command before the *Victoria*'s next voyage.

Nome old-timers were said to have gone aboard clutching large bouquets of flowers, or gingerly holding boxes purported to contain bonbons. It was suspected that these farewell tokens would gurgle if shaken.

And then there were the stewards who went ashore at Cordova, returned to the ship just as she was casting off, and had to jump to the Jacob's ladder to climb aboard. As they made the leap, sprays of bottles issued from their trouser legs and went splash-splash-splashing into the water — bottles of bootleg liquor intended for sale to thirsty passengers. Intended customers, leaning over the rail to watch the late boarders, let out a collective groan as the bottles sank.

Another time, a steward from steerage on the *Northwestern* dreamed up a get-rich-quick idea. He had observed that Indians in the cannery towns were easy marks when it came to investing in liquor, so he brought north 80 bottles of cold tea and, at Hoonah, announced that he would sell some choice whiskey at five dollars a bottle in the last quarter of an hour before sailing. Buyers, he stipulated, must bring the exact change and agree to leave the ship without sampling the contents. He sold out his stock completely, made $400 in profit, but didn't dare go back to Hoonah.

One captain said that when he sailed on the *Jefferson* as quartermaster in 1922, the crew kept a barrel in a locker and manufactured wine in it, helping themselves to raisins and prunes from the cargo. "The barrel was so popular," he said, "that the passengers came down to patronize it."

Alaska Steam had a long-standing arrangement with the Alaska Railroad for the "Golden Belt" tours. Since construction days an affinity had existed between Alaska Steam and the railway; their first joint through-tariff became effective in 1922. For years they joined to promote travel with coordinated schedules to serve vacationers. They advertised loop trips in which some passengers went inland at Seward and others at Valdez, visited Fairbanks, then came out at the opposite port. Bus service was available at the Valdez end and train at Seward. Prior to the end of World War II the railroad did not operate at night. Everyone got off and stayed in a comfortable roadhouse at Curry, and breakfasted there in the morning before continuing the train journey. In summer, this was a curious custom because daylight lasted almost 24 hours. After the war the trains ran straight through.

The Golden Belt tours were comparatively cheap and a great attraction. "You had to have your ships on schedule," explained Sid Hayman, former manager of advertising and public relations for Alaska Steam. "One time a steamer arrived at Valdez to pick up a party and a flood had washed out a bridge a few miles inland. We rigged a pulley and board for passengers to sit on and brought them across from the bus. One woman refused to get on. The purser volunteered to go across and hold her in his lap. The double weight made the board sag to the ground and wore a hole in the seat of his pants."

In 1920 the company ordered a new type of vessel built at the Todd shipyard in Seattle; a twin-screw motor ship, the first oceangoing craft to use heavy crude oil in her diesel engines. The *Kennecott*, 3,620 tons, was 469 feet long, cost $1,200,000 and could travel at 11 knots. Her operation was economical; she could load 5,000 or 6,000 tons of ore compared with the freighter *Latouche*, which carried only 2,400 tons.

The *Kennecott* made eight voyages to the Atlantic Coast before Alaska Steam scheduled her to carry ore. Capt. Ludwig

Tour buses to the Interior of Alaska departed▶ from Valdez on a regular basis.

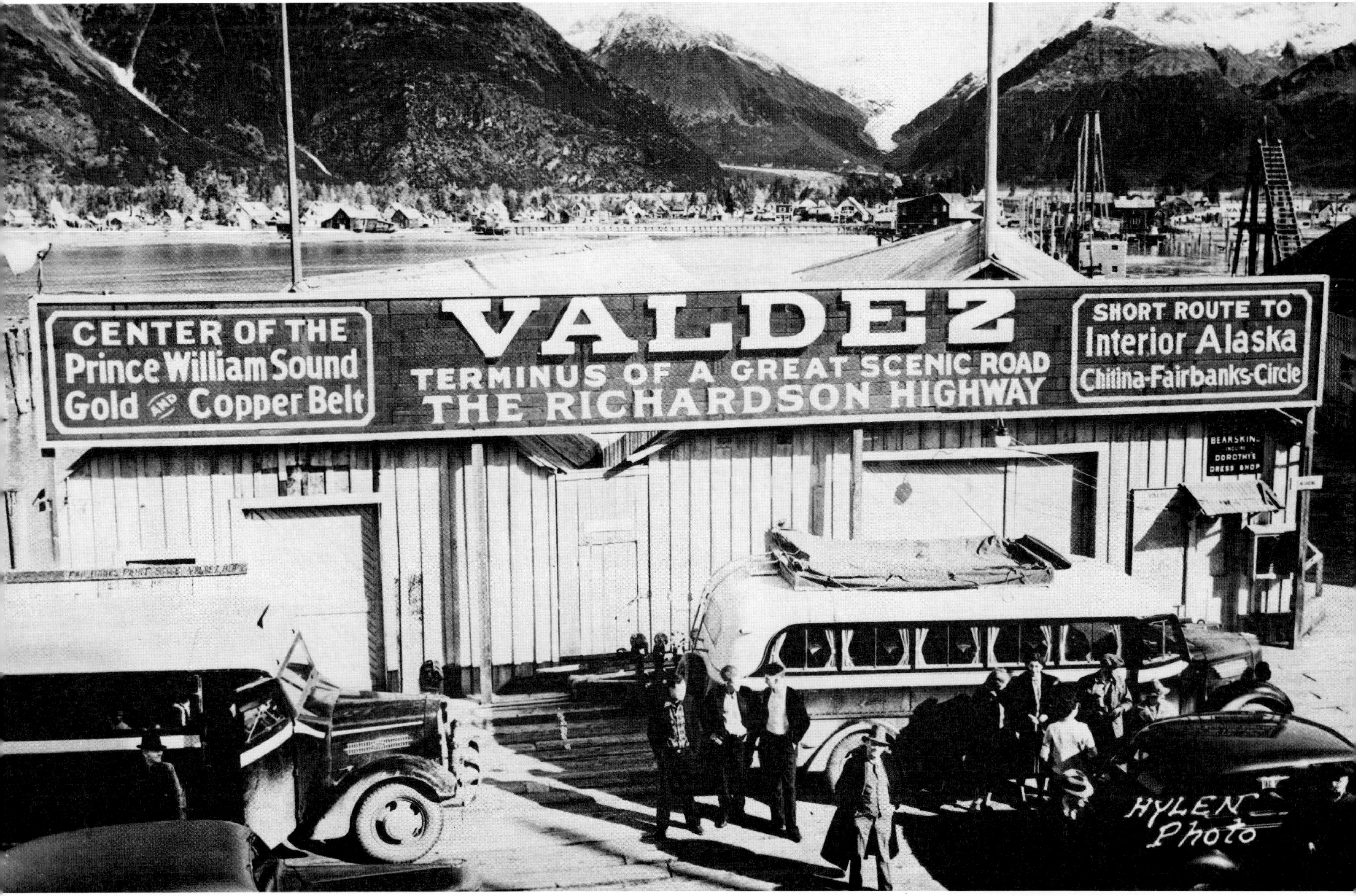
VALDEZ
TERMINUS OF A GREAT SCENIC ROAD
THE RICHARDSON HIGHWAY
CENTER OF THE
Prince William Sound
Gold AND Copper Belt
SHORT ROUTE TO
Interior Alaska
Chitina-Fairbanks-Circle
HYLEN
Photo

SS Kennecott
Joe D. Williamson

72 □ Alaska Steam

Jacobson was aboard as third mate on her first trip with lumber to New York. He liked her because everything aboard was fresh and new.

On her initial voyage with copper as cargo she sailed under Capt. John A. "Laughing Jack" Johnson, from Seattle to Yokohama. She arrived there two hours after the terrible earthquake of Sept. 1, 1923. She also called at Kobe, then sailed for Seward to clear customs before going to Latouche to pick up concentrates. From the latter port she departed for Tacoma, but on Oct. 9, off Hunters Point, Graham Island, in the Queen Charlottes, she ran aground. No lives were lost, but the ship had to be abandoned. The crew went ashore by breeches buoy. At first it was thought that the *Kennecott* could be salvaged, and the tug *Algerine* was rushed to the scene. Unfortunately the tug struck a rock, was seriously damaged, and could not rescue the freighter. The *Kennecott*'s million dollar cargo, consisting of 6,000 tons of copper and 40,000 cases of salmon, was lost with the new vessel.

Captain Johnson, then sixty, brooded over the loss of the *Kennecott*. She was his second shipwreck. His first, years earlier in Finlayson Channel, was the *Ohio*. En route to Victoria aboard the *Algerine* after her failed rescue effort, as the ship neared the scene of his earlier disaster, Capt. Laughing Jack Johnson leaped overboard to his death.

In 1921 the Alaska Line inaugurated service to the Hawaiian Islands with once-a-month sailings of the *Cordova* to Honolulu and Hilo and a call at Astoria, Oregon. The *Cordova* had only 18 staterooms, none with private bath. The service did not pay off, so was discontinued at the end of the year.

SS *Kennecott* with a breeches buoy rigged.

In September of 1922 Alaska Steam purchased the freighter *Medon*, 3,474 tons, from the U.S. Shipping Board and rechristened her *Oduna*, the name of the Indian woman who had befriended the prospectors who located the Kennecott copper deposits.

As freighting to the North increased, Alaska Steam needed larger freighters. Early in 1923 the company sold the small cargo ships *Juneau* and *Valdez* to a company operating on the Great Lakes. The *Santa Ana*, which had been idle for three years, was sold for the Kuskokwim River trade, and the *Skagway*, for lumber carrying. Other craft were purchased to replace them. In April 1923, the *Delrosa*, a sister ship of the *Oduna*, was bought from the Shipping Board and named the *Tanana*. The *Lake Gebhardt* was acquired in San Francisco shortly after, but was wrecked off Destruction Island on May 9. The company immediately purchased a replacement, her sister ship, the *Lake Filbert*, which was renamed *Nabesna*; she remained in service until April 1928.

In June 1923, the Todd shipyard completed the new passenger liner *Alaska*, the second ship of that name. She registered 4,658 gross tons and measured 350.4 by 15.6 feet. She soon became known for her fast runs from Ketchikan to Seattle. After turboelectric power was installed in 1932 she covered the distance in 39 hours and 56 minutes.

Complaints about the high cost of shipping to Alaska again resulted in rate hearings, in 1923. The inquiry served to emphasize the handicaps under which Alaska Steam operated. Business was

◀SS *Alaska II*

The cover of an Alaska Steam brochure promoting the luxury of visiting Alaska.

SS Yukon

extremely irregular. During peak seasons the company was forced to charter three additional vessels for two-month periods. In early spring, however, before traffic began to canneries and salteries, there was not enough southbound traffic to fill one steamer a month, except for the usual ore shipments. This slack time generally lasted one-third of the year.

Besides information on the wide fluctuation of cargo, the hearings produced clarification of Alaska Steam's preferential rates to canneries. Special freight rates for tin plate, tin cans, box shooks (bundles of short boards), cooperage and cordage encouraged the canneries to utilize the steamship line instead of chartering other ships. For the same reason freight prices were lowered for a pulp mill at Snettisham, near Juneau.

The year 1924 saw another passenger liner added. She was the *Colon*, purchased from the Panama Railroad Company and rechristened *Yukon*. She was brought from the Panama Canal by Capt. C.A. Glasscock, who was to remain her regular master for many years.

In 1925 the company's method of placing cargo on ships was improved. For years cargo had been loaded onto two-wheeled hand trucks in the warehouse and pushed to the ship's side, where two men filled net slings. This required four men; two to load the hand trucks and two to load the slings. The new method involved loading a large square-board sling at the pile. An electric lift truck then hoisted it and took it to the ship's side, where it was picked up and put on board without repiling. This effected a 40 percent saving in labor.

The next vessel to be added to the fleet, in September 1925, was the freighter

El Capitan, renamed *Lakina* and assigned to the cannery trade on the west coast of Prince of Wales Island. She and the *Cordova* served canneries exclusively during the fishing season, because it was found that sending the large passenger boats to the fisheries in southeastern Alaska not only caused much delay but brought complaints from passengers. A good many pleasure travelers did not enjoy the odorous atmosphere around such places, although the company folders coyly termed the cannery stops "Surprise Ports." Later passenger accommodations were added to both the *Cordova* and *Lakina*.

October 1925 saw the end of the *Jefferson*. That old reliable steamer went to the scrap heap. (Later her bell was given to the Puget Sound Maritime Historical Society.)

Before the close of the year the company purchased two more vessels from the Shipping Board, the *Depere* and the *Jeptha*, rechristened *Denali*. Two vessels were to bear the name *Denali*; this was the first.

The last of five sister ships acquired in the course of three years was the *Derblay*, built at Oakland, California, in 1920 and purchased the following February from the Shipping Board. She had been assigned to the west coast of South America, with the General Steamship Company as agent. When the sale was completed she was adapted for lumber transport, and passenger accommodations were added so she could transport workers to canneries, salteries and whaling stations. Under the command of Capt. John Newland she usually made at least one annual trip to Kotzebue and Nome. During winter seasons she often chartered to other lines to haul lumber.

By 1925 the Morgan-Guggenheim syndicate had shipped $175 million worth of copper from Alaska. From 1915 through 1928 the value of copper production in the Territory exceeded that of gold.

The boom in copper ore was running strong in December 1926, when Alaska Steam purchased the *Panama* from the Panama Railroad Company. She was renamed the *Aleutian* after extensive remodeling for the northern trade, but she was not destined to be long on the run. In February 1929 she hit Maude Island in Seymour Narrows and disabled her steering gear. She managed to back off the rocks and proceed south, but near Waldron Island in the San Juans she anchored after developing a bad list. The *Alameda* took off her passengers before she continued to Seattle. A soldier on board became so crazed during the excitement that he cut his throat with a razor. He was overcome by seamen, given first aid, and placed in a straight jacket for the remainder of the voyage.

A little more than three months later, on May 30, in broad daylight and a calm sea, the *Aleutian* struck a reef off Amook Island, near Kodiak. It was Captain Nord's first wreck in thirty years as a master in Alaskan waters. The last passengers barely got away in lifeboats before the stern went up. One woman escaped in her nightgown and coat and had to jump from the rail. She was hauled aboard a lifeboat as the ship went down. Air pressure in the *Aleutian*'s last moments sent a gush of towels and clothing out of portholes many feet into the air. The only loss of life was that of Manuel Dorras, a janitor, who went back to his room for his lucky horseshoe.

Help came from several sources. Some hunters with a gas boat took women and injured persons to the cannery at Larsen Bay. The Coast and Geodetic Survey steamer *Surveyor* hastened from Zachar Bay when the SOS sounded, and found a cannery tender towing lifeboats with some of the crew. The *Surveyor* provided hot food and medical attention for minor injuries, and also picked up the rest of the survivors and took them to Seward.

Captain Nord's license was suspended for sixty days. The *Aleutian* was off course at the time of the accident and the rock was marked on the latest charts.

Tony R. Dressel of Kodiak recalled, "I found an old man who saw the *Aleutian* go on the rocks from his father's fox farm on a nearby island. He said she had taken a 40-foot rip in one side, but the captain fully expected her to float when the tide came up. When the tide did rise she slid stern first off the rock to the bottom of a 47-fathom hole beside the rock. A barge and divers were brought in immediately to try and salvage her, but due to the limitations of diving equipment of that time, they were unable to reach her."

Halton N. Peterson, chief clerk in charge of freight bookings in 1917, remembered, "Before the *Aleutian* struck, her next sailing was to have been the last Saturday in May, with a full load of Shriners from Cleveland.

"At 5:30 a.m. on the Monday prior to the scheduled sailing I received a phone call from Shriner Clarence Allen saying, 'What in the hell did you do with my ship?' I told him we had sunk her and were going to refigure the schedule to take care of his party. We had three ships on the Seward run, giving us a three-week turnaround with a sailing every Saturday. This gave the ship a four- or five-day

The first SS *Aleutian*.
Joe D. Williamson

78 ☐ Alaska Steam

lay-up between sailings. We held a meeting and found that by cutting lay-ups to two and eliminating cannery calls we could sail a ship every Sunday morning, providing weekly service with only two ships. We managed to rebook the entire Shrine party on the *Alaska,* sailing Sunday morning instead of Saturday and giving them rooms with bath and meals Saturday at the Frye Hotel, at our expense.''

Within months the company replaced the wrecked *Aleutian* with the *Mexico,* previously owned by the Ward line. She had been launched at Philadelphia in 1906. When the Alaska Steamship Company purchased her she brought to the Pacific Coast new boilers for the *Alaska* and the *Victoria* as well as some machinery to be used in her own remodeling. The name *Aleutian* was given to this second ship. She measured 400 by 50.2 by 22.4 feet; her gross tonnage was 6,361. She was completely rebuilt at West Seattle at a cost of a million, and was considered the best-fitted and most spacious ship of the fleet. She had 14 deluxe staterooms with twin beds, tub and shower, and a capacity of 334 first-class and 162 steerage passengers. The dining salon seated 160 at a time. Her maiden voyage north was May 3, 1930. That month she carried a Seattle Chamber of Commerce businessmen's excursion, and in June the Los Angeles Chamber of Commerce booked her for a party.

The end of the *Alameda* came in December 1931. She had just come in from the North and had not yet gone to Tacoma to discharge her ore cargo at the smelter. Early in the morning, as she was lying at Pier 2 in Seattle, fire broke out on board and gained headway so fast that the

The SS *Alameda* on fire in Seattle.
Joe D. Williamson

ship, ablaze from stem to stern, had to be towed away from the wharf and beached at the entrance to the East Waterway. Two seamen who had been asleep were rescued by firemen. There was no loss of life, but the 415 tons of copper in the hold were lost.

In April 1933, an agreement was entered with the Pacific Steamship Lines Ltd., which in 1916 had succeeded the Pacific Coast Steamship Co. as the firm's chief competitor. The Great Depression had affected the Pacific Lines' coastwise business severely; operating costs had mounted because of higher wages and better working conditions. For years Alaska Steam had had a built-in southbound copper cargo, but Pacific Steamship's boats were obliged to return empty except during the salmon season.

Alaska Steam paid its competitor $300,000 to get out of the Alaskan trade. By that time most of the boats owned by Pacific Steamship, which had been purchased by the Dollar Line, were running elsewhere or had been sold for scrap. Alaska Steam took over the *Curacao,* which Pacific had used in a feeder service out of Kodiak, and kept her until 1938, employing her in shuttle service out of Cordova.

Bob Rose remembers a sidelight on the Alaska Steam-Pacific Steam deal. "When the changeover was taking place," Rose said, "A.F. Haines, who headed the Dollar organization, sent a teletype message to the management, saying, '*Admiral Watson* arrived in Seattle, net revenue $5,000. I still say we made a big mistake.' Haines didn't want to see the [Pacific Steamship] line sell out."

As part of the arrangment, Pacific Steamship insisted upon the right to send the *Dorothy Alexander* on the Alaskan cruise each year. Five years later Alaska Steam took over the *Dorothy,* and changed her name to the *Columbia.*

Alaska Steam still had competition on the Alaskan run. The Canadian Pacific and Canadian National railways each had a vessel, or vessels, on the run between Vancouver, British Columbia, and Skagway for many years. There was also the Northland Transportation Company, launched in 1923, competing with Alaska Steam for the Alaskan trade for 25 years.

In March 1934 Alaska Steam acquired the *Dellwood,* already a familiar vessel in Alaskan waters, where she had served as a cable ship. At the time of purchase she belonged to P.E. Harris and Co., a salmon canning firm.

The SS *Dellwood* after being refitted for the Alaska Steamship Line.

Inset: The SS *Dellwood* in her earlier life as a cable ship.

Puget Sound Maritime Historical Society

CHAPTER

Depression Years

When one explores the early history of Alaska Steam, very little information comes to light on labor problems. Labor relations appear to have been amicable. Only a few disagreements are recorded. A short strike was staged in 1906. In 1907 a fight took place on the *Dolphin;* the man involved was fired and the crew struck. Indians had to be employed to work cargo in southeastern Alaska, but the Skagway longshoremen refused to work with them. It was quite a problem to get a shipment ashore and the boat under way.

Unique among strikes was the one described in a 1916 clipping preserved by Chief Steward G. "Jack" Dillon. The scrapbook item, headlined *Underdone Chop Delays Big Ship,* tells how the sailing of the *Northwestern* was held up seven and a half hours. The firemen on board were having dinner when one of them, Joe Thomas, bit into a mutton chop that was cooked rare and still bloody. He

◄Cannery workers waiting to board the
Cape Victory in Seattle.

made uncomplimentary remarks to the waiter, who retorted that he had neither cooked the chop nor killed the sheep. The fireman took the offending segment of meat out to the galley where Phil Duncan, the big Black cook, held forth. The latter was polite, but when the fireman uttered a string of oaths the cook struck him on the nose. A fight followed and the fireman staggered into the dining hall, announcing that his union had been outraged. The other firemen got together and informed the chief engineer that if the cook was not discharged they would quit. The captain was notified and he in turn sent word of the mutiny to the manager. Meanwhile, when a conference was called, a delegation from the cooks' and stewards' union backed the cook. It was decided that he was entitled to defend an invasion of the galley. The firemen finally consented to go back to work, but insisted that all chops must be well-done in the future. The company officials acclaimed Duncan as the best cook in the service, and announced that they did not intend to part with him.

Until 1934, labor troubles were of minor

UNDERDONE CHOP DELAYS BIG SHIP

Alaska Liner Northwestern Held Up Seven Hours and Thirty Minutes While Fireman Wrangled With Cook.

PEACE CONFERENCE SETTLES CONTROVERSY

Galley Lord Pleads Unwritten Law in Landing Swing on Coal Heaver and Is Upheld by Board of Arbitration.

An underdone mutton chop caused a delay of seven hours and thirty minutes to the steamship Northwestern, which left Seattle for Alaska Saturday night.

While the anchor was being weighed to see if it was heavy enough to make the trip, and the compass was being boxed, the firemen of the big steamship were having dinner. The menu consisted of mutton chops, green peas and plum duff.

The chop served to one of the firemen was a bit underdone. As he cut into it, the blood flowed, and then he began to say things. The waiter swelled out his chest and said that he had neither killed the sheep nor grilled the chop, and he did not propose to stand for a call-down.

The fireman grabbed the bleeding crop and strode to the galley where big Phil Duncan, so black that charcoal would make a white mark on him, holds forth. The fireman swung the gory chop aloft and wanted to know what the cook meant by sending such stuff to the firemen's mess. The black cook used diplomatic language. It had the wrong effect.

The fireman thought he had the cook bluffed, so he cut loose with a string of oaths that made the foreman of the gang of longshoremen on the dock curl up in envy.

Black Cook Gets Peevish.

Then the cook got peevish and pasted the fireman on the nose. The blood of the fireman mingled with that of the chop, as they rolled together on the deck of the galley. When the fireman succeeded in brushing the dream stuff out of his brain he staggered into the dining hall and announced that the dignity of the firemen's union had been outraged by a son of Ham.

An executive session of the firemen's protective association was immediately assembled and a committee was sent to inform the chief engineer that if the cook was not discharged the coal heavers would quit. The chief engineer passed the word along to Captain Trowbridge. The captain hitched up his trousers and megaphoned to Manager Trowbridge that the firemen had mutinied.

Then there was a gathering of the clans. The officers of the company, the captain, the outraged fireman and the cook assembled at the conference. Purser Triggs was cast in the role of the white-winged dove of peace.

Pleads Unwritten Law.

Cook Duncan, his black face shining like polished ebony, pleaded the unwritten law. He was backed up by the walking delegate of the cooks' and waiters' union, who was hastily summoned from a pinochle game to safeguard the right of the cook.

After every man having anything on his mind was given a chance to relieve the pressure, it was decided that Cook Duncan was clearly within his rights in defending an invasion of his galley. The firemen were still sulking, but they finally consented to go back to work, but issued an ultimatum that chops must be well done in future, or they would strike again.

The peace negotiations took considerable time, and the Northwestern finally tooted farewell and headed for the north seven hours and thirty minutes late. As

---

Mutton Chop Is Cause of Delay In Ship Sailing

An underdone mutton chop delayed the sailing of the steamship Northwestern seven and one-half hours last night. The ship was due to leave port at 2 o'clock yesterday afternoon but it was 9:30 p. m. before the lines were cast off. The Northwestern boasts of a colored cook, Phil Duncan. Phil is king of the galley but yesterday noon he grilled a mutton chop which offended the epicurean tastes of Fireman Joe Thomas. Joe raved and tore his hair. He rushed to the galley and confronted Phil with the offensive dish.

"Look here, you son of darkness what do you mean by insultin' me with a mutton chop like this?" fumed the enraged fireman.

"Doan you want it?" asked Phil mildly.

"No, I don't, you blackberry pie," shouted the fireman.

"Then take this," said Phil, handing the fireman a left hook to the jaw.

After Joe woke up he stumbled to the stoke hole and called a council of war. Seven other firemen attended the indignation meeting.

"Fellow firemen," quoth Joe, "shall we tolerate this insult from that coon in the galley? Shall we pass up this attempt to end my earthly career?"

"Nix and no," shouted the assembled firemen.

Forthwith a delegate was authorized to lay the facts before the captain.

"Discharge the cook or we quit," announced the delegate.

"Never," said the captain.

The matter was then taken before the walking delegate of the marine firemen's union who repaired to the offices of the Northwestern Steamship Company. The company refused to part with Phil's services, claiming that he is the best cook in the service.

After several hours' debate both sides compromised and the firemen agreed to shovel coal on the trip to Valdez.

The Northwestern is carrying a full cargo of freight and a fair passenger list.

importance to the Alaska Steamship Company. Job control was vested in the ship owners and open shops prevailed. After World War I there had been some unrest in the maritime unions. By 1920 the government had lost interest in maintaining labor peace in the shipping industry. Wages were reduced, speedups were required, and overtime was almost eliminated. In May 1921, a nationwide seamen's strike was called, but the masters and mates did not recognize the action and stood by Alaska Steam. The main difficulty was in obtaining engineers, but some came out from Cleveland and Chicago and broke the strike. Itinerants without sea experience were shipped as sailors on some vessels, and strikebreakers were obtained for other departments. The strike action ended in August 1921, when representatives of the unions agreed to return for the wage scale offered. Open shop was to exist from 1921 until 1934. The seamen enjoyed little prosperity and felt the full impact of the Depression when wages were reduced to about half their 1921 levels.

Employees did not have much choice about what they did in the early years. During the Depression they were accustomed to being called on for a variety of labor. F.W. Ross described conditions when he started with the company in 1931:

It was difficult for a fellow to get a berth before the days of the sailors' union.

One had to know a mate. About March they'd start breaking out the boats that were laid up during the winter at their berth in West Seattle. That was when you boarded a streetcar, went out there, waylaid a mate at the gate, and got him to sign you on. I used to make the summer run for six or seven months and then sail offshore in the winter with some other line. It was like a vacation for me on those winter runs, because we worked four-hour watches. On the Alaska Line we'd go three or four days, with sleep only during lunch hours or for very short periods.

You see, we did maintenance work, weather permitting, then we worked aboard ship four to six hours while we lay in some small port, then went right on watch after that. The runs were short and there might be only an hour or two after we went off watch when we had a chance to catnap before another port. If a fellow complained he was tired, they'd have a replacement for him the next trip, so you kept still about it.

One made a good deal of money, however, because the crew worked the cargo for extra pay. If there was a shortage of crew to make up two cargo gangs, we recruited steerage passengers to get enough men. In the days before the 1934 strike, longshoremen were not organized.

We'd pull into Juneau and handle gold concentrates. The freighters mostly handled the copper ore out of Cordova and Latouche, but occasionally the passenger vessels took on ore if a lot was ready at the dock. The sacks were so heavy you always had a man on each end, one hanging onto the tie-off and the other taking the bottom corners. The salmon cases were cartons weighing about 50 pounds each. You had to stack them closely up to a height of nine feet. After a few hours of that without a break, you knew you'd been working.

William L. Taylor said it was a good deal the same in the purser's office, where he was freight clerk. "It was drudgery — cargo books and manifests were all kept by hand. There were no typewriters or adding machines. On the southeastern run we worked night and day, Seattle to Ketchikan."

During the depression years the West Seattle yard furnished employment to Alaska Steam crews during the winter months. Capt. Robert W. Nordstrom of Edmonds was a mate in those days. He told of working as a pipefitter's helper and as a night watchman during the slow months. "We needed lots of watchmen when the fleet was laid up," he recalled. "The company gave many of us winter jobs, but later the unions made them cut that out. We could stay on, however, as a watchman or mate standing by on shipboard. By then pilots and captains had retainer pay when ships were laid up."

With so many men available in winter the company's repairs were made mostly by its own employees instead of being contracted out.

Commencing in May 1934 labor relations changed greatly after an 83-day strike tied up the Seattle waterfront. The company's business came to a standstill; northbound supplies were not allowed to travel to Alaskan. Through the interven-

Patsy Ann, the pit bull terrier always seen on the Juneau docks when the ships came in. The story went that her master left town on a boat and never came back. She survived on handouts from the men working in the ships' galleys.

tion of the Secretary of the Interior, longshoremen permitted ships with emergency cargo to depart. In this way the *Victoria* was released. Although an agreement was reached with the unions, the company refused to fire 70 men who had remained loyal through the strike. This called for more arbitration. What peace was achieved was an uneasy one, and for several years there were continual maritime labor crises. They did not end completely until the declaration of World War II.

A glamourous vessel appeared on the Alaska run in 1934, when Alaska Steam chartered the *Haleakala*, which the Inter-Island Co. had been operating in the Hawaiian Islands. She carried 334 first-class passengers and 100 third-class or steerage. She was well-equipped for the trade except that no provision had been made for heat in the cabins.

Helen L. Ball of Seattle recalls:

Few trips I have taken could match the glamour and thrill of my voyage in the Haleakala *to Alaska in 1934. A labor strike nearly doomed my plans for adventure in the North, but the management of Alaska Steam managed to lease a Hawaiian ship and arrange a sailing from Tacoma right on schedule.*

In those days sailing was a colorful event. The departees were well-supplied with confetti and streamers. A crowd of friends would be on the dock and excitement mounted until the whistle blast signaled the final departure.

A large group of my friends made the trip to Tacoma to see me off. One of them had a florist concoct a special bouquet for the occasion. The centerpiece was a large cauliflower surrounded by radishes, carrots and leeks. It was handed to me over the rail and caused much amusement.

The passengers were a friendly group. Among them were three girls from Springfield, Illinois, with whom I teamed up. We were dubbed The Four Horsemen and were ready to make the most of every day. At Petersburg a U.S. Navy submarine was tied at the same dock. It didn't take us long to make the acquaintance of a couple of her sailors. After answering some questions about their quarters, they offered to take us below to see for ourselves. We were just climbing down when an officer appeared. It was evident the two sailors were in for a bad time. We were hustled out of there in short order.

After the *Haleakala*'s first trip to Alaska brought complaints about the chilly cabins, the company installed electric heaters in the passenger quarters. She was taken off the northern run at the end of the season, after only three months' service.

In 1935 there were changes in the company fleet again. The *Starr* was purchased from the San Juan Fishing and Packing Company in April and in December the *Redondo* was scrapped.

The catastrophe of the year occurred in May 1935 when the *Denali*, in a heavy sea and dense fog, hit a reef off Zayas Island, near Prince Rupert, British Columbia. The *Denali* had a full cargo of freight,

SS Mount McKinley
Joe D. Williamson

There's always a Santa at Christmas. Flanking him (left to right) are Ken Cross, Capt. Joseph Ramsauer, an unidentified child and G.S. "Cowboy" Duryea.
Skinner Foundation Collection, Alaska Historical Library

including 30 tons of dynamite. Fire broke out, then the ship split in two and sank except for her bow, which remained on the reef. Capt. T.E. Healey and all on board were saved by the Coast Guard cutter *Cyane.*

In January 1936 Alaska Steam acquired the *Mount McKinley,* the former Grace liner *Santa Ana.* The next month Grace also sold the *Santa Elisa* to Alaska Steam; she was renamed the *Baranof.* These were large vessels designed for the tourist trade. In January 1938 the company made one other purchase of this type, a Grace liner, the *Caracas.* She was renamed *Denali.* In May 1936 the *Arthur J. Baldwin* was purchased from the Lomen Reindeer Co. and renamed *Bering.* Lomen had used her for carrying reindeer carcasses from the Arctic Coast.

F.W. Ross, who was second mate on her at one time, recalled, "She was loaded with bedbugs and when I came home to Seattle some of them came with me. In a night or two my wife was complaining that something was biting her. We had to fumigate the whole place."

A company folder in 1936 listed the Christmas ship as an annual attraction, offering a 16-day trip, with 10 ports of call and a chance to help Santa Claus. R.C. "Bob" Rose described it:

I don't know exactly when it started, but each year the company arranged that a vessel would sail early in December, on a schedule that included practically every port of call in Alaska, as far west as Kodiak. There was Santa Claus on board, and the ship carried the customary three-piece girl orchestra. We also hired some professional entertainers for this cruise.

In Alaska it was well-known when the Christmas ship was on her way. Long lines of children waited to come aboard at every port.

It really was a beautiful thing. Kay Kennedy wrote a story about a miner on the Richardson Highway, who loaded his little daughters on a sled and took them to Valdez to see our Santa Claus. Alaska was far more isolated then that it is today. For a child, a chance to see Santa was a great treat.

In 1937 the *Sutherland* was purchased and the *Nizina* was sold. The *Columbia* also joined the company fleet that year. She was assigned to passenger runs. Capt. Reuben Jacobson was mate on her. He became master and remained with her five years.

On April 30, 1937, the *Cordova,* while she was in a gale on Hecate Strait, had to send out an SOS when fire broke out in No. 2 hold and the steering gear malfunctioned. At the time she was under the command of Capt. J.D. Goetz. The Coast Guard *Alert,* the USS *Swallow* and the *Northwestern* rushed to her assistance. Finally the flames were smothered and next day the *Cordova* reached Ketchikan safely.

On Oct. 1, 1938, during a heavy fog, the *Yukon,* with Captain Glasscock in command, outbound with 113 passengers, and the *Columbia,* inbound with 252 passengers, both traveling at full speed, collided off Jefferson Head. Both ships were severely damaged, their port bows and superstructure stove in. The port anchor and chain of the *Columbia* were embedded in the crumpled bow of the *Yukon.* After the accident they got into Seattle under their own power.

William L. Taylor, freight clerk on the *Yukon,* described his shattering experience during the collision. "Lifeboats were flying all over and the ships were scraping equipment off the sides of each other. A fireman was killed instantly. Captain Glasscock felt terrible about it. In those days there was no radar or fathometer and the captains still sailed by instinct."

In 1938 the Guggenheim syndicate terminated its copper shipments. Bob Rose, then a new employee of Alaska Steam, described the end of the Guggenheim era. The Kennecott mine staff was to pull out for keeps in the final days before the annual spring washout of the Copper River and Northwestern Railroad bridge at Chitina. This structure went out with the ice and had to be replaced at once. "There was much careful planning as to moving men, machinery and whatever items were to be salvaged," Rose said. "Everything was being done on a prearranged schedule those last few weeks. Then suddenly the company hit some fantastically rich pockets in the mine, and the question became whether to bring out copper or machinery. It is my recollection that they decided to take the copper and leave the equipment. I'm not sure the story about this ever leaked out. We figured in the decision, because Alaska Steam acted as traffic manager for the railroad."

The Cordova agent said that nobody around town really believed the railroad era was ending; they thought the mine was closing only temporarily, so it did not come as a great shock to the residents.

F.W. Ross tells about an experience aboard the freighter *Latouche.* "It was after the Copper River and Northwestern Railroad closed and equipment was being taken out," he related. "We were 24 hours loading the locomotive and tender on deck. The *Latouche* was a well-decker and the locomotive was on a trestle and lashed to the bull rail.

"Pretty soon on the gulf we got into a southwester and the ship began to roll. I was at the wheel and I could see the engine move a little. After about 10 rolls, wham, she went through and took out the bull rail on the port side. I thought we were going over with her. We lay over, then snapped up and righted. The tender didn't go overboard."

Only salmon was left as the southbound cargo. Sometimes, after Kennecott closed, ships had to be rushed north empty or held in standby status to load. The ships relieved the limited cannery storage facilities so the lines of canning machinery did not have to shut down.

Bob Rose described some of the problems. "Perhaps three times as many canneries as exist today were spread along the Alaska shoreline. Some were almost self-supporting for waterborne transportation, operating ships of their own. But most depended upon us. Their labor traveled steerage; the executives, first class. Getting them all north at the precise time they wanted to be there was always a bit of a problem. The cannery people were well aware of the amount of accommodation on our ships and the fact that there might be more demand than space available. So it was necessary to prorate the space among the canneries. Some asked for more than they needed, figuring that when prorated they would be cut down to what they wanted."

The Great Depression was coming to an end as war clouds gathered in Europe. In June 1940 the *Curacao* was sold, in August the *Starr* went and in September the *Northwestern* left the fleet.

CHAPTER 7

The Alaska Line Goes to War

World War II was to have great impact on the Alaska Steamship Company. Between 1940 and 1942 a new state of affairs materialized in the North, the rise of what one author has called "Military Alaska." The era of copper was over, like that of whalebone, canned salmon, gold and fur shipments, and the remaining sources of cargo were on the decline. It took a war to pour new life into Alaskan transportation.

In 1939 only 524 military personnel were stationed in the whole Territory of Alaska; of these a large number were operating the telegraph and cable service. By July 1943, service personnel had expanded to 152,000. Starting in 1940 the Navy developed bases at Sitka, Kodiak and Dutch Harbor. Later the Army arrived in Anchorage, Cold Bay, Umnak and Fairbanks. In early 1941 a tremendous movement of cargo began.

"Alaska Line schedules were upset by this," explained Bob Rose. "We fell so far

◄ **Dutch Harbor, Alaska, February 1942.**
Puget Sound Maritime Historical Society

behind we reprinted the sailing schedule three times in 1941. We had to deal with angry passengers all over the country. They would show up on a certain date and find no vessel sailing. Meanwhile we'd be pleading with the Navy to unload our boats.

"A Navy contractor got the *Yale* from the Matson Line and took her to Kodiak to use as housing for workmen; at Sitka the *City of Victoria* was secured for the same purpose, and the *Northwestern* was towed to Dutch Harbor. The latter was also to supply power. She had been laid up about 1937 and sold in 1940 because she was getting too old.

"Turmoil reigned the last year before war was declared. Passengers and cargo were going everywhere. When the war started, Alaska Steam became an agent for the War Shipping Administration and was assigned back its own ships to operate with some additional government-built vessels."

A disturbing time was in store for both passengers and crewmen. A Cordova resident remembers sailing from Seattle two days before Pearl Harbor. When the

Getting out of the way of a war: evacuees in 1942.

steamer arrived at Ketchikan it received orders that it was to be painted gray and wait for a convoy. No passengers nor crew members aboard were allowed to communicate with their families to explain the delay.

F.W. Ross, a boatswain in those days, told of coming down from Seward on the *Yukon* when war was declared. "We had orders to run into Yakutat, where the Army had an outpost, and to go no farther. We had been stopping there previously, taking on supplies. We were to await further notice about Japanese submarines, so we waited three or four days, all the time receiving radio reports about a steam schooner that was helpless in Unimak Pass. While we sat it out, a submarine surfaced out there and shelled the schooner and its lifeboats. Meanwhile we were trying to take fresh water aboard as our supply was running low. It was December and the water line froze. A steam line had to be played on the hose to keep it open."

The aged *Victoria* was called out of retirement. The obsolete ship had been laid up for several years; now she was to be converted into a freighter. A newspaper article hailed her as the world's oldest ship. She was in her 80th year and had worn out only one engine. Her hull of Swedish iron, with frames 14 inches apart and plates one and one-eighth inches thick, was very unusual.

At the beginning of the war the company had 16 vessels of its own; 60 others were assigned to it. Of the entire fleet of 76 ships under its direction, only four ships were lost. Here is what happened to some of the vessels in Alaska Steam service during the war years.

November 21, 1941 — Cordova

refloated after grounding on Woody Point, Chatham Strait, badly damaged but able to proceed south. She was pulled off the reefs by two Coast Guard cutters and an Army Transport Service vessel and the passengers were removed.

December 1941 — The *Lakina* evacuated women and children from the U.S. Naval Base at Kodiak because of danger of attack. The *Cordova* evacuated those at Dutch Harbor.

March 1942 — The *Kenai* was sold, the first vessel delivered to the government under operation by the War Shipping Administration.

March 18, 1942 — The *Mount McKinley* stranded on a reef at Scotch Cap at the entrance to Unimak Pass, following the zigzag course ordered by a naval convoy commander during a submarine alert. Passengers, cargo and mail were removed safely and it was hoped the ship could be salvaged. She was high and dry at low tide but storms came up and pounded her to pieces before she could be refloated. She was one of the line's large vessels, 5,000 tons gross, measuring 373 by 51 feet 6 inches.

July and August 1942 — The *Oduna, Depere* and *Tanana* were requisitioned and sold to the government. All the ships in the company fleet were delivered by June.

July 19, 1943 — While laying fire-control cable between Attu and Shemya in the Aleutian Islands the *Dellwood*, commanded by Capt. Lars Erickson, struck a submerged pinnacle and sank. One lifeboat filled with survivors was nearly hit by the starboard anchor when it was accidentally released. A cook jumped from a lifeboat to a Navy sub-chaser, missed, and fell into rough water.

A naval officer jumped in and rescued him. No loss of life occurred. Purser Robert C. Wilson succeeded in saving all the ship's funds and payroll records.

April 19, 1944 — The *John Straub*, one of the assigned vessels, under command of Capt. Axel W. Westerholm, disappeared between Scotch Cap and the mainland and was thought to have been torpedoed. She was carrying a cargo which included explosives for the military, so there could have been an internal explosion. All hands were lost.

April 27, 1945 — The *Canada Victory*, another of the Alaska Line's assigned ships, was lying off Okinawa with a full load of ammunition when she came under enemy fire. A Japanese kamikaze plane crashed onto the after gun tub, tearing off the stern of the ship. Fortunately the cargo did not explode. The ship settled by the stern and the crew stepped off into the water. An assistant engineer, three Navy gun crew men and a cadet officer were killed. The vessel came to rest on the bottom with her mast protruding above the surface. Later, due to an ammunition shortage, divers descended, cut open the ship, and recovered some of her cargo.

Another report said that the gun crew of the *Lew Wallace* knocked down two Japanese planes.

Capt. Adolf "Big Dan" Danielson was on a series of three Alaska Line boats carrying ammunition and troops to the South Pacific.

"I was commanding the *Richard Mansfield*," he said. "We were traveling in a convoy without lights, when we collided with a naval vessel off Unimak Pass. My ship wasn't damaged; we were the ones who ran down the PT boat. I

stopped and waited until daylight, picking up men and trying to find four who were missing. I hope to tell you it was tough navigating without lights in the Bering Sea."

Captain Danielson was also on the *Terre Haute Victory* and the *George Flavel*. When his ship carried ammunition it had to travel without a convoy. He often saw the masts of sunken vessels sticking out of the water, but he was never attacked. In his long career he said he never had a wreck.

Capt. Raymond Dowling remembered, "On convoys in wartime we'd have several escort ships. Sometimes next morning not a vessel could be seen anywhere. The weather was so bad it would take all day to get the entire lot of ships back into position. Once an old coal burner, the *Otsego*, was in the convoy and several times she sent up clouds of sparks and smoke. Right after that the commander would order us to scatter, and then we'd have difficulty getting assembled all over again.

"It was tough traveling up the Inside Passage in black weather when you were going 14 knots, knowing rocks were right over there and we had to depend on echoes.

"What was my most exciting time? When I was on the *Baranof* we hit Hein Bank beyond Port Townsend, in a fog, with a full load of troops on board. We damaged seventeen plates, tearing seven of them out of her. We turned right around and went into dry dock. As soon as the *Baranof* was up all the oil drained out of her into the bay. What a mess that was!"

Capt. Ludwig Jacobson said that during the war he landed 300 Navy recruits one evening at Dutch Harbor and refused to wait around because it was too dangerous there. The next morning, June 3, 1942, when he was at sea, he learned by radio that the Japanese had bombed the port and killed some of the men he had brought. He was captain of the *Columbia* when the pilot ran her aground north of Alert Bay, toward the end of the war. She was stranded 13 days before they got her off. During wartime Jacobson said he used to go to bed partly dressed, ready to go on deck at any time.

Douglas R. Renbarger described the Alaska Line's attempt at secret code. "Our ship captains were generally always associated with the same vessels, such as Jock Livingstone, the *Northwestern*; Gus Nord, the *Aleutian*; Hans Odsen, the *Denali*; Glasscock, the *Aleutian* and later Joe Ramsauer, the *Baranof*; Nilsen, the *Denali,* etc. This was so standard that when censorship was inaugurated in 1942 we wired our agents in Alaska, for example, "Ramsauer departed 0900 and will see you Monday." This plainly indicated that the *Baranof* had departed Seattle on schedule. This seemed like a foolproof code against the Japanese and worked for a while. Bob Rose, our passenger department agent, was moved into active service from the Navy Reserve to head the Navy censor's office in Juneau and, after a few months, advised us to cease and desist. Everybody in Alaska knew Ramsauer was captain of the *Baranof*, and by this time the Japanese must have known it too. We could have switched to using the chief purser's name, but they, too, were generally associated with the same ships; for example, Red MacNamee with the *Aleutian*; Frank Bartlett, the *Northwestern*; Bill Hickman,

the *Denali*; and Dave Doran, the *Alaska*."

Travelers remember how run-down the ships became during the war. On the *Aleutian* the draperies were tattered and the windows boarded up, guns were up forward and no lights were allowed after dark.

The wartime conflict still raged in August 1944, when the Alaska Steamship Company changed ownership. The Skinner and Eddy Corporation bought the line's assets for $4,290,000. Since 1930 Gilbert W. Skinner and two associates, Bill Semar and Ray Anderson, had owned the Northland Transportation Company, which offered the major competition to the Alaska Line in southeastern Alaska. The third competitor was the Alaska Transportation Co., owned by Norton Clapp, which ran the *Taku, Tyee* and *Tongass* in the same part of the Territory.

Northland was the older of these two competing firms, organized in 1923 by Seattle men headed by William Semar. Its first boat had been the *Bellingham*, none other than the Alaska Line's old *Willapa*. Northland did not provide any service beyond southeastern Alaska until just prior to World War II, when it began calling at Kodiak and Sand Point. Although the line solicited passengers, the company's primary interest was the southbound movement of frozen fish.

Gilbert Skinner had other interests in Alaska. In 1926 he had organized the Alaska Pacific Salmon Company. His father, D.E. Skinner, had been a partner in the Port Blakely Mill Company and had moved into shipbuilding in 1916. The son became president of Skinner and Eddy in 1932. He had a passionate regard for ships and, anticipating a resumption of private operations in the North after the war, he

took steps to do something about it. Knowing that the fleets of both Northland and Alaska Steam had been depleted, he proposed to Lawrence Bogle, a vice-president and general counsel for Alaska Steam, that Northland's remaining vessels be sold to that company or that Alaska Steam be purchased from the Kennecott Copper Corporation.

Kennecott's original interest in the line had been to provide transportation for its copper ore, but by this time the corporation no longer had its own product to transport out of Alaska, so it had good reason for approving the sale. A secondary consideration was that there had been many problems created by the war and Alaska Steam's role as agent for the War Shipping Administration.

After the sale of the company to Skinner, in November 1944, W.E. Brown returned from the War Shipping Administration and became operating manager of the line. Besides the transfer of the fleet, the purchase by Skinner included the West Seattle ship repair facilities, the Ketchikan Wharf Co. and the Lake Washington shipyard. The assets were transferred from the Nevada corporation to a Washington corporation.

During its years of operation Alaska Steam actually owned 66 ships. Numerous others were used under lease or charter. With the end of the war in August 1945, Alaska Steam's fleet of 16 vessels had shrunk to one third that number. In addition to wartime casualties, five ships had been sold to foreign countries because of their age and high market value at the time. One ship sold late in 1945 was the old Lomen veteran, the *Bering*.

SS *Derblay* dressed for war. Note the ▶ gun "tubs."

CHAPTER 8

Postwar Problems

T he end of the hostilities did not bring an end to government control. In the 1945 season the company still operated 12 cargo vessels under bareboat charter from the Maritime Commission. The vessels remained under charter from the government until 1949. During the postwar period Alaska Steam eliminated stops at Wrangell, Petersburg, Haines, Skagway and Sitka. Instead, Northland served that run every two weeks, using the steamer *Alaska*. When the Maritime Commission finally returned the vessels to their original owners, Alaska Steam got back only the *Baranof, Aleutian, Alaska, Columbia, Denali, Lakina* and *Cordova*, and the freighters *Derblay* and *Sutherland*. Northland received two R1-M-AV3-type vessels, the *Lucidor* and the *Palisana*, and a Liberty freighter, the *Chief Washakie*.

Bob Rose said of the early postwar period, "The ships were returned to us in bad shape. They had been run constantly and hard, with a minimum spent on

◀**Pier 42 in Seattle, circa 1950.**

passenger accommodation maintenance. When we got them back we painted them, fixed them up and went after tourists. We got out manuals and distributed them to travel agents throughout the country and to railroad offices."

Amid the new literature was a little booklet entitled *How to Be a Salt*, containing a ship's vocabulary, descriptions of departments and instructions on how passengers could relax and make themselves at home. It stated that there would be no need for formal attire, but men were asked to wear ties and coats in the dining room, and the tourist advice noted, "Women customarily do not wear slacks or shorts to dinner." It also mentioned the traditional ship's concert and advised travelers to see the purser about it and get into the act. It also noted that firearms had to be checked with the purser, and subtly pointed out that, "When you're cruising the placid waters of the Inside Passage, you might want to consider some of the problems your captain faces. He must pass through Seymour Narrows at 'slack water,' which occurs approximately every six hours. Otherwise, the water would be

How to be a Salt, a pamphlet to help passengers appreciate the seagoing adventure.

so turbulent the ship could not be adequately controlled." It mentioned that Wrangell Narrows must be traversed "when the tide is near its highest point, and if your ship calls at Sitka, you may pass through Sergius Narrows and Peril Strait — if the tide is just right — otherwise you are taken around Cape Ommaney or through Icy Strait." The slogan printed on this folder had changed from "Sailing Sheltered Seas" to "See America first, but start with Alaska."

Artwork for posters and other advertising materials was splashy. Eustace P. Ziegler became virtually an in-house artist for the company, and the paintings he was commissioned to make were copyrighted and became widely known from their use in national publicity. He was a friend of E.T. Stannard, formerly supervisor of the Kennecott mine and superintendent of Alaska Steam. Sydney Laurence also made several paintings for the company. Artists Nina and Josephine Crumrine designed a set of dog portraits for menu covers, which were available as souvenirs. Every effort was bent to attract tourist trade.

Syd Hayman spoke of Westours and how they became a big operator in the North. "Chuck West got out of the Air Force and went to work for the Wien airline. From that he got into his own tour agency in Fairbanks. When we started our tourist service in 1947, we found there were almost no hotel accommodations in Fairbanks. We had to refuse to take tourists bound for Anchorage and Fairbanks unless they had obtained confirmed hotel reservations. After that we began to hear from people who said they had reservations from Arctic Alaska Tours, which we had never heard of. On

"CHEECHAKO"

Some of the artwork commissioned to spruce up the steamship line's appearance.

The *Yukon* after her stern had broken away.

investigation we found that Chuck West had set up army tents and army cots for them. We got hold of West and talked with him. After that we assigned him staterooms. He built a hotel business on ability and sheer hard work."

Rail travel was still popular and the company paid commissions to railroad agents and travel agents for tickets sold. Rose explained, "Northern Pacific had remarkable connections with all kinds of groups who traveled each summer. Several radio stations promoted Alaska cruises. We also signed on many religious groups. The Northern Pacific would get in touch with a hundred or so of their members, book them on a train, and send them to Alaska Steam. We would set aside a block of rooms and hold them 30 or 60 days in advance of the sailing. This resulted in large numbers of round-trip passengers.

"Another thing we did to keep passenger ships in service year-round was to enter a contract with the military; we carried a substantial number of persons to Seward, destined for Fort Richardson and Elmendorf Field. Toward the end of our service the Army became so unreasonable in its demands that this simply did not work out."

Rose remembers postwar rush seasons when a couple of thousand cannery workers had to be moved to Bristol Bay. The U.S. War Shipping Administration assigned the company some large troop transports such as the *Young America* and *Cape Victory*. Their steerage bunks were five high, military-transport style, and their so-called first class consisted of rooms with bunks three high.

Capt. Raymond Dowling has some postwar memories of his time sailing aboard the *Cordova*, a single-screw oil-burner with a steel hull and double bottom. "We were warned about her by an old pilot, who said you had to watch her," Dowling reminisced. "In the winter of 1946 we were heading toward Kodiak from Cape Spencer, got into a storm, and couldn't steer. The *Cordova* wallowed broadside into a sea and couldn't get her head up again. We were rolling, the main deck was under, and we were icing down. We were halfway across the gulf when the bad weather hit us. We couldn't go back. Finally, after trying an hour or so to get up speed, we managed to turn the stern into the sea. The ship rolled like a duck then, but we could take that. We had to wait two days until the weather quieted. Meanwhile we were out there all that time, rolling around, unable to go any place.

"The *Cordova* was a cranky ship. Another time when we went around Turn Point No. 2 on Prince William Sound, she wouldn't straighten out and made a turn round in a complete circle. I complained after that and the shops gave her more rudder angle, so we had no more trouble.

"I remember my first trip as skipper on her. We waited for slack water in Seymour Narrows and then got caught in a tide rip. The ship veered over and headed for Maude Island Light. I thought I'd be walking home. When we were 50 feet from the light we finally got the *Cordova* to veer off again into deep clear water. Up to then I'd been scared stiff. This was before we had radar on the ship."

Early in 1946 the company fleet suffered a heavy loss. The *Yukon*, still under charter from the government, was on her southbound voyage with 369 passengers taken aboard at Seward on Sunday afternoon, Feb. 3. A blinding snowstorm and strong northeast wind overtook her that night. Capt. Chris Trondsen could not pick up the light at the end of Elrington Island. He ordered a change of course; the ship's whistle blew constantly. In spite of these precautions, about 4 a.m., she bumped aground on a narrow, foam-lashed beach close to cliffs. Because it was very dark, as far as anyone could see it looked as though the ship was stranded about fifty yards from land. Heavy seas made it impossible to launch boats on the offshore side, so it was thought safer for all persons to remain on board until daylight. The engine room flooded immediately.

At daybreak it was ascertained that the wreck had occurred near Cape Fairfield. The Coast Guard cutter *Onondaga* was sent to the rescue from Montague Island. Huge seas were still running and a crack appeared between the smokestack and the bridge deckhouse, causing fear that the vessel would split in two. When a lifeboat attempted to reach the beach and rig a breeches buoy, it was swamped.

The cutter arrived at 12:30 p.m. and some passengers were put in her whaleboat and a lifeboat. Before the whaleboat could return for more passengers, the *Yukon*'s stern broke away. The remaining passengers huddled near the forward gun tub. At 3:30 p.m. a mighty sea carried 21 men over the side. Four were washed up onto the beach and two were carried back on board. An Army power barge picked up about ten others.

On hand were the *Cedar* and the *Curb*, a Navy salvage tug, but they could not get close because of pounding seas. Army bombers parachuted provisions and life rafts to the section of the *Yukon* that remained intact. There were still 480 men and women aboard wearing bulky life jackets, gathered in the social hall, on the bridge and in the officers' staterooms; all available space was crowded. Meanwhile, 40-foot waves were jarring the ship on the rocks and more cracks were developing.

Another night came on, with all the rescue ships standing by, their floodlights turned on the *Yukon*. Five more boats joined those already in the rescue group.

In the morning a line was fired on board and a life raft was attached. Two more lines were rigged later and the slow process of removing passengers began. A fourth line was put aboard and the shuttling speeded up. Sometimes rafts capsized and people were tossed into the sea. The rescue went on all day, but the task was not yet finished by nightfall. More than 100 persons were taken off by breeches buoy on a line rigged ashore. Bombers dropped sleeping bags onto the beach. Attempts were made to parachute provisions, but these fell into the water. The passengers stranded ashore had only a few potatoes for food and, to add to their misery, it began to snow during the night. Next morning this group on shore was directed to a sandy beach farther up the bay. Here a power barge picked them up.

Eleven persons were lost; five civilians and six soldiers, who had been among the lot washed overboard. Captain Trondsen was the last man off the *Yukon*. He got away in a rubber raft at two o'clock on the third and final day of the rescue.

———————

The year 1946 was a grim one for the company, marked by many interruptions of service caused by labor unrest. Bob Rose, former vice-president of traffic for Alaska Steam, kept a diary which recorded the difficulties:

April 17, 1946 — All ships idle. Sailors Union demanding deluxe room for quartermasters in *Alaska*. Sailors Union demanding company fire mate in *Aleutian* — overtime dispute. Alaska longshoremen on strike — retroactive pay dispute. Filipino cannery workers picketing. Cooks refuse to obtain new War Shipping Administration competency cards; therefore cannot sign on.

April 20 — Longshore strike in Alaska settled. Ten ships scheduled to sail. Filipino cannery workers start picketing at midnight.

April 21 — Tied up by Filipinos.

April 23 — Filipinos agree to permit freighters only — no cannery cargo.

April 27 — Seattle cannery workers accept industry's offer. Alaska unions now preventing operation.

April 30 — Alaska cannery workers settle — nine ships scheduled. Stewards and firemen voted to strike on or after May 6.

May 6 — CIO unions meeting in San Francisco asked by [Harry] Bridges to vote for strike as shipowners policy now "imperialism and war."

May 23 — Railroad strike effective 4 p.m.

May 24 — Railroad strike settled.

June 15 — No work on waterfront. CIO voting on new agreements.

June 28 — Longshore strike Ketchikan and Juneau.

July 10 — Embargo on Juneau.

July 13 — Embargo on Juneau ended.

July 15 — Seattle longshoremen stop work.

July 16 — *Denali* originally scheduled 17th, postponed 18th.

July 17 — Still tied up by longshoremen. *Denali* postponed to 19th.

July 20 — *Denali* sails.

July 23 — *Lakina* postponed to 27th.

July 30 — Longshore strike at Juneau ties up *Baranof*. *Alaska* overtakes *Baranof* at Juneau. *Alaska* rerouted Seward-Seattle direct after completing present northbound voyage.

Sept. 6 — Pickets, sailors union, at all docks. All work suspended. Notified passengers and agents sailings indefinitely postponed.

Sept. 13 — Sailors' pickets withdrawn. Picketed by firemen and National Maritime Union. Stewards taking strike vote tonight.

Sept. 21 — Press reports strike ended. All unions agree to return to work, having been granted all demands.

Sept. 23 — Longshoremen at work, but no sailors.

Sept. 25 — Still no sailors. Working *Oduna* for Bristol Bay and *Victoria* for Nome with standby crew.

Sept. 28 — The two ships sail.

Oct. 2 — Committee for Maritime Union agrees to allow *Cordova* to sail for Nome, taking balance of cargo left by *Victoria*.

Oct. 7 — *Cordova* sails for Nome. Pickets return to Pier 50. All work stopped.

Oct. 24 — No change. Occasional threats by union members required office workers to obtain union dock passes, but no interference at Piers 50 and 51. Press reports union will clear relief ship for southwestern, southeastern ports, food-stuffs only.

Nov. 19 — CMU agreed to release relief ship *Grommet Reefer*. Commenced to accept cargo.

Dec. 9 — Seattle waterfront reopens.

Dec. 27 — Longshoremen at Seward demanding to do winch driving aboard ship. Sailors refuse. *Baranof, Denali* and *Reef Knot*, all idle at Seward.

Dec. 31 — Seward longshoremen announce they will discharge the three ships under protest.

For months Rose jotted notes about railroad strikes, no work on the waterfront while the CIO voted on new agreements, longshore strikes in Ketchikan, Juneau and Seattle. Some ship sailings were postponed and others rerouted. Between June 1946 and February 1947, the *Sutherland, Columbia, Derblay, Cordova* and *Lakina* were sold.

On Aug. 13, 1947, the company was involved in the largest collision loss ever experienced on the Pacific Coast. The *Diamond Knot*, under bareboat charter to Alaska Steam from the Maritime Commission, was en route from Bristol Bay to Seattle with 154,416 cases of choice salmon from three packers. Her tanks held 50,000 gallons of herring oil; on deck were 155 barrels of salted fish, an automobile and a tug. The 5,525-ton freighter entered the Strait of Juan de Fuca in fog and choppy water and met the 10,681-ton freighter *Fenn Victory*, riding high and making for the open sea. They collided three miles off Race Rocks. When rescue tugs found them the *Diamond Knot* had a great slash in her starboard side and her decks were awash. The high bow of the *Fenn Victory* was entangled in the heavy crosstree of the *Diamond Knot*'s mainmast and the two ships were in a death grip. They were finally cut free when the crew from the rescue tug employed acetylene torches. The *Fenn Victory* ran for port. The *Diamond Knot* was taken in tow so she could be beached, but she got into strong currents and sank half a mile from Crescent Bay. Later the vessel and her cargo figured in a spectacular salvage operation.

Farther north up the coast the *Denali* was the first vessel to reach the scene of one of the region's worst maritime disasters. The Army transport *Clarksdale Victory* ran full speed ashore on a reef on the west side of Graham Island in the Queen Charlotte Islands. The transport broke up under a terrific pounding and efforts were made to search for the crew. The *Denali* almost lost several of her men in unsuccessful attempts to land them on Hippa Island to look for survivors. On their return to the ship a giant wave splintered their small craft against the *Denali*'s hull, dumping eight men into the sea. They were rescued and pulled aboard safely.

It was late 1948 before the Alaska Line got back to normal after six years of government control. Until 1947 the company had scheduled its Seattle sailings from Pier 51, formerly called Pier 2, but now it moved to the new Pier 42, specially designed for the Alaskan trade. The structure was built where a shanty town had stood until it burned in 1941. It was also the location of the Skinner and Eddy shipyard. The new pier had been used by the Army and Navy during World War II. When it was assigned to the Alaska Line two buildings were added; a steel structure for repairs and an office building. Another facility made available to the Alaska boats for use as a winter lay-up was the shipyard at Houghton on the east side of Lake Washington. It was purchased by a subsidiary, the Alaska Terminal and Stevedoring Company.

Improvements were made in the vessels themselves. Alaska Steam was one of the first commercial fleets to be equipped with radar, an important asset in the treacherous northern waters. The SS *Alaska* received radar license No. 1, but there was no general use of radar until after World War II. A new safety element was added to the shipping lanes of the North, one that had long been needed.

The SS *Tatalina*, formerly the *Square Sinnet*.
Joe D. Williamson

104 ☐ Alaska Steam

The Decline of Passenger Service

After the war, barely enough business was generated in Alaska to support one steamship company. Residents complained constantly, blaming high freight rates for the increased cost of living in the Territory, even though other factors were responsible. In January 1947, the territorial legislature sent a memorandum to Congress charging that "the discrimination of the Jones Act in favor of a few rundown Puget Sound ships" was blocking movement of goods and passengers, and had been obstructing Alaska's development for "over 30 years." This charge did not take into consideration that Alaska's population had declined after the war, nor that cargo tonnage was further decreased by the banning of fish traps in 1948. (This ban ended the heavy shipments of wire and piling that had been used in trap construction.)

Because the nature of Alaskan trade required that a great number of small, unprofitable ports be served, early in 1947 the Maritime Commission wanted Alaska shipping operators to form a single company to eliminate duplication of service and costly competition. Federal assistance was to be withheld unless this was done. In spite of this, four competitive companies serving Alaska hung on a little longer. An interim plan was put into effect in which the government provided the needed ships for one year, at nominal charter-hire cost, ending in July 1948. The plan's termination coincided with a three-month-long West Coast shipping strike.

At the conclusion of this period, with Alaska returning to prewar conditions, a single company was regarded as the only economical and efficient means of servicing all of the Territory. G.W. Skinner, president of Alaska Steam, said there was barely enough business for one firm. In many ports it was difficult for a single company to make ends meet, and there were few places where two lines could operate at a profit.

Although an effort had been made to effect every possible economy and avoid an increase in rates, the first three months of 1949 showed a heavy loss. The rates had to be increased, or the interim plan reapplied. The outcome was that the three other carriers discontinued their Alaskan operations.

Alaska Steam never had invaded the Kuskokwim River country, which was strictly the province of the Santa Ana Transportation Co. Santa Ana retired from the river trade by degrees after the termination of government aid. At first Alaska Steam provided a ship and crew, while Santa Ana continued to run the operation. After a year Alaska Steam took over, employing a CI-M-AV1 shallow-draft motor vessel to get into the river and off-load at Bethel.

"It was an expensive way of handling cargo for Natives, prospectors and fishing enterprises," said Rose. "We took in three ships a year. We'd bring out empty containers from Bethel and pick up frozen fish on the way past some of the other westward ports. You had to have the CI-M-AV1s well-trimmed so as not to hit mud in some of those places. Sometimes they had to anchor at the mouth of a river and let scows handle the cargo. At each of these places we had to pick an agent and warn him what his troubles would be."

Capt. Robert Nordstrom recalled ten years on the run to Bethel in such ships as the *Susitna*, *Galena* and *Tatalina*. "We ran 135 miles up the Kuskokwim from Goodnews Bay and got stuck in the mud every trip," he said. "We never went up without getting stuck someplace, but we would wiggle around and get through. On the spring trip we had full loads and went up with the tide. Lots of times we had to anchor 11 miles below Bethel and discharge 700 or 800 tons before we could move. Bethel is a distribution center for the mines upriver that keep that country

going. Smaller barges and river tugs took the stuff we discharged. Our arrival on the Kuskokwim was something like Christmas for the people around there."

Back in Seattle, changes took place in the home office. W.E. Brown had been transferred to the post of general freight and passenger agent and in the spring of 1948 he died. J.F. Zumdieck succeeded him as operating manager. G.S. Duryea then became general freight and passenger agent. In January 1950, D.E. Skinner was appointed vice-president and general manager.

In July 1948, the *Terminal Knot* was purchased from the government and renamed the *Susitna*. The company had previously employed her on a charter basis. She was the first of the postwar acquisitions, a vessel 321 by 50 by 21 feet, commanded by Captain Nordstrom.

In March 1949, the company bought the assets of the Northland Transportation Company, including the *Chief Washakie* (later called the *Chena*) and the yacht *Leonore*. By 1949 four Liberty ships and four Knot-type vessels had been purchased. The use of unitized containers was initiated. Although Alaska Steam did the largest volume of business in its history in 1949, it sustained a loss of $53,106 in spite of a period free of labor problems. From December 1948 to July 1950 the company handled grain cargoes from Pacific Coast ports to the Orient under contract to the Army, employing the Liberty ships *Harold D. Whitehead*, *Peter J. McGuire* and *Edmund Mallet*. In 1951 the firm bought the *Mallet*, 7,198 gross tons, and renamed her *Iliamna*. The *Dorian Prince* was purchased and renamed *Nadina*.

A news item dated July 24, 1950, tells of a fire aboard the *Coastal Monarch*, the Alaska Line's lone ship scheduled to call at Kotzebue Sound ports that year. (The *Coastal Monarch* was on charter from the Maritime Administration from 1948 to 1967 and never was owned by the company.) She caught fire off Sand Point, flames appearing when a hatch was opened. The Coast Guard cutter *Sweetbriar*, on her way to Adak, went to the assistance of the ship and finally succeeded in quenching the blaze before it reached the cargo of gasoline. When the fire was out the *Coastal Monarch* had to turn around and go back to Seattle, so Nome did not receive its shipments.

Jack Dillon, then in his first year as agent at Nome, recalled, "I had to go around and tell our clients, 'You didn't get your freight, but you still owe us for it.' They didn't understand the principle of general average. If they didn't have insurance on their shipment they were out of luck." As a result of this experience the company later included in its rate insurance for the benefit of the owner of cargo.

When the Korean War broke out the company became involved in delivery of war materials. From August 1950 to February 1952, several government-owned vessels were operated on a per diem basis under contract to the Military Sea Transportation Service. These were the *Honda Knot* (a CI-M-AV1 or small Knot-type freighter), the *Clovis Victory*, *Bedford Victory* and *Joliet Victory*. During the push-back of United Nations forces late in 1950 the *Joliet* barely missed enemy action. She was discharging at Inchon, Korea, when she was ordered to reload and clear promptly for Yokohama. Later she was ordered to

**The SS Chena (formerly the Chief Washakie)
tied up at a cannery near Ketchikan.**
Puget Sound Maritime Historical Society

A typical CI·M·AV1, a shallow-draft motor
vessel. This one is the *Flemish Knot*. Note
the numerous cargo booms.
Skinner Foundation Collection, Alaska Historical Library

discharge her cargo at Moji. On either side of her were other Victory ships loading prisoners of war.

Labor relations had not improved. There were constant work interruptions, demands for pay raises and less work performed per man.

Bob Rose's diary records the line's difficulties:

April 15, 1950 — *Square Knot* sailed with cannery cargo for Kodiak Island ports. Fishermens Union notified company ship would be picketed. Picket line. Cargo not discharged and ship ordered back to Seattle fully loaded.

May 10, 1950 — Embargo on all cannery cargo. Cannery workers threaten to picket any ship loading cannery cargo.

Oct. 6, 1950 — *Baranof* had to sail as freighter, no passengers, because of stewards' dispute.

Nov. 3, 1950 — First passenger sailing.

Nov. 10, 1950 — *Denali* sails without incident.

Oct. 18, 1951 — *Denali* had to call at Whittier instead of Seward because of longshoremen strike.

Shortages of longshoremen caused sailing schedules to fall apart and costs skyrocketed with abnormal detention of vessels. Ships loading Army and Navy cargoes got first choice in assigning the longshoremen, leaving commercial carriers to those who were left.

In the spring of 1950 Alaska Steam was charged with driving out competition in an antitrust case. The company volunteered free access to its records. The indictment accused Alaska Steam and five of its officers of attempting to acquire a monopoly in transporting people and commodities by water in the Alaska trade and of coercing shippers to use its facilities.

In a company newsletter, the management accused Gov. Ernest Gruening of being the instigator of the grand jury investigation and monopoly charge. The company spokesman said that the Territory's water transportation problems could have been satisfactorily dealt with long ago, had it not been for Gruening's unrelenting agitation, obstruction and noncooperation to every plan presented. Gruening introduced a bill that would have tied Alaskan shipping to the apron strings of the Interior Department. It was feared that his constant attacks would result in degeneration of private service to the extent that the government would step in, seize the ships and socialize the industry. He constantly harped on the theme that Alaska Steam was committing what he termed "seaway robbery."

Charges against the company and the officers were dismissed by a federal district judge in September 1952. Meanwhile, with increasing costs, rates went up and rate hearings upheld them.

A marine cooks' and stewards' union strike late in 1950, and a sailors' union strike in May 1952, tied up operations and cost the company much revenue. During the sailors' strike the voyages of 13 passenger ships and 15 freighters were canceled; 2,550 northbound tourists were unable to sail, freight losses exceeded $2,750,000 and stevedoring wages were lost at both ends of the runs. Still another strike occurred late in 1952 when only relief ships went out.

Bob Rose recalled details of the strikes:
On one trip of the Alaska *the full load of 220 passengers were on*

Governor of Alaska Ernest Gruening
Alaska Historical Library

board and people were standing at the rail waving good-bye when the steward's department walked off. The ship had been scheduled to sail at 5 p.m., the dinner hour was approaching and there she sat with no cooks and no bakers — a real mess! About 5:30 it became obvious that we would not have stewards, so I started shopping around for a restaurant that would take the passengers for dinner on very short notice. After a good many calls I finally got the old Frye Hotel, where they kept a large supply of canned hams on hand, and it agreed to accept the passengers if they would eat this entree. Of course we had a few people among the passengers who could not accept this, but the hotel promised to produce some fish. So we chartered Grey Line buses — four of them — and carried all the passengers to the Frye, where dinner was served at our expense. Then they were brought back to the ship.

This was when the stewards' union was under Communist control and was thrown out by the other unions. When we got back to the ship we found that the stewards had left a mimeographed sheet in every stateroom telling what a bunch of dogs we were and saying, among other things, that the president of our company had been a millionaire draft dodger during the war. The fact was that he had served on a destroyer through World War II

and had seen plenty of action.

Some of the strikes we went through were called at the last minute. You never knew what to expect. When we had definite knowledge that the ships were not sailing we endeavored to get word to passengers, but by the time the telegrams were sent, the passengers were usually on their way. It was my duty to stand at the gate of Pier 42 on sailing day, meeting people as they drove in and telling them they weren't going anywhere. Men would get mad and want to punch me in the nose, and women would burst into tears. We refunded the ticket money in full, of course, and tried to help everyone out on the vacation most of them had planned for a long time.

Alaska Steam was the political whipping boy for certain politicians and newspaper editors, a distinction it shared with the Seattle Chamber of Commerce and the canned salmon industry. Attacks certainly did the company no good. I remember Bob Atwood, who had the largest Alaska paper, The Anchorage Times. *He was a fine, able and intelligent gentleman, but he never had a good word to say about Seattle.*

At that time Alaska Steam published a map for free distribution, which was perhaps the best and most detailed map of the Territory from any source. One year it became necessary to run off a new edition. At our Pier 42 head-

quarters we asked employees and visitors to check the map and see what had been omitted so we could include it in the new edition. We compiled a list of villages and islands and sent the whole thing off to the printer. When the first few thousand were delivered somebody in our office looked at the new map and noted that, while we had added everything anyone could think of in Alaska, we had omitted Seattle. We made the correction. It so happened that I was on my way to Alaska on one of my regular trips, and I took along some of the copies which omitted Seattle. In Atwood's office I told him we were well aware of his opinion of the city. When he saw the map, he thought it was wonderful. As far as I know, it is still hanging in his office.

In 1952 the old *Vic* (*Victoria*) came out of lay-up and left for Seward with 525 tons of seed and fertilizer for the Matanuska Valley Farmers Cooperative. She was the oldest vessel flying the American flag, but she went into temporary retirement again at the end of the season.

On July 26, 1952, in the midst of the strikes, the *Baranof* collided near Nanaimo with the *Triton*, a Greek steamer loaded with iron ore, killing two persons on the Greek vessel. It was the worst accident on the line since the sinking of the *Diamond Knot*, besides being a blow to the tourist season already complicated by the 53-day seamen's strike. The *Baranof*, with a tarp lashed over the hole in her bow, went into Vancouver to land

SS *Baranof*, after her collision with the Greek *Triton* near Nanaimo.
Puget Sound Maritime Historical Society

passengers before returning to Seattle. This cut short a cruise for 150 vacationers.

Bob Rose recalled those tense weeks. "It was bad enough the way labor troubles tied us up tight," he said. "We were trying to catch passengers before they left home to tell them of the strike. The week after the strike was over we had a Presbyterian cruise booked on the *Baranof* when it had the collision. We had all those people who weren't going anywhere. The *Baranof* brought them to Vancouver on a Saturday when no banks were open. We drove up there to handle the situation; $30,000 to $40,000 had to be refunded to the passengers. Getting the money was a problem, but our agent found a suburban bank that was open on Saturday morning. He brought back mail sacks full of cash. I took a sack to the boat and explained that Canadian dollars were worth more than American and asked the passengers if they would be satisfied to take the refunds in local currency and go where they wanted. They were more than willing to do it."

Another of Rose's memories of church tours relates to an annual Methodist Alaskan cruise. "We carried the Methodists for several summers, arranging a round-trip with a special calendar of events and assigning them the whole ship. The Methodists said, 'We want the bar closed.' Under union rules we had to carry the bartender, so we told them, 'If you fill the ship we'll put him aboard as a passenger.'

"Sailing day came and three staterooms of non-Methodists remained, so we said, 'We'll have to open the bar.' One of our three extra passengers was a radio announcer. He was given the darndest farewell party you ever saw. The Reverend Gould, who handled the Methodist cruise, was furious about it, but there was nothing he could do."

After air travel became popular the Alaska Line ran only one ship a week north in winter, but in summer the line operated four passenger vessels.

On July 9, 1953, travelers aboard the *Aleutian* witnessed a sight not listed on the advertising folders. The ship ran into a dusty cloud on Turnagain Arm. It was like entering a tunnel. Mount Spurr, 80 miles west of Anchorage, was erupting, spewing volcanic ash.

The *Seattle Post-Intelligencer* quoted an Edmonds woman, Helen MacKenzie, then an Alaska Steam employee in Anchorage. She recalled seeing the volcanic activity at Mount Spurr and Mount Torbert. She said the town was blackened with smoke and ash from the Territory's "most spectacular volcanic upheaval in years."

"It was dark at noon on a sunshiny day," she said. "Everyone was covered with ash. It looked like you were on the moon. One smart guy bagged the ash and sold it for a dollar a bag."

In October 1953, G.W. Skinner died suddenly of a heart attack at the age of 54. His son, D.E. Skinner, vice-president and general manager of the Alaska Line since January 1950, succeeded him as president.

Several improvements were made in the company during the season of 1953. Teletype equipment was installed in all agencies, and containerization, with its elimination of unnecessary cargo handling, was started experimentally.

Before the firm was fully into containerization it began in a small way with a corrugated steel cargo guard for handling fragile and highly perishable merchandise, dock to dock, between Seattle and the approximately 65 ports the company serviced. This guard, four by six by six feet, stood on legs to facilitate lifting; it was filled and sealed at the dock. Another early device was a small wooden crib, to be filled by shippers and delivered to the dock. Guards could be stacked outside the warehouse, but cribs and pallet loads had to go inside. These early methods of containerization represented a beginning, but they were soon to become outmoded.

The Alaska Line unwillingly contributed a lot of building material to Alaskans as the result of this effort. Many of the four-by-eight-foot plywood tops of the cribs were pilfered, later to be seen patching walls and sidewalks up North.

After World War II, the old methods of piece-by-piece moving became too expensive. A new concept in container-barge service was developed. Containerized cargo was carried by forklift and placed at the edge of the dock, then a forklift on the barge lifted it from the dock and stowed it on the barge. When discharging from the barge, the operation was reversed.

By the next year, 1954, container handling was large-scale; it proved to have advantages in cutting pilferage, loss and

Containers began to see common usage. Here a Gard is lowered through the 'tween ▶ decks to the lower hold of the *Susitna*. Notice the lifting hooks in the eyes at the upper corners. Also note the flexible duct used for forced ventilation when the forklifts were in use below decks.

A trip to the New York World's Fair in 1939. Artist Robert Mayokok and his family, at the invitation of New York Mayor LaGuardia, traveled from Cape Prince of Wales as representatives of Alaska.

damage. It also allowed good temperature control which retarded the ripening process of fresh foods, hence ensuring the delivery of perishables in better condition. Another improvement was the pioneering development of rate calculation by computer.

The company continually experimented to find better ways of doing its jobs. Operating costs were becoming extremely high. Getting necessities to a population of 200,000 spread over 586,000 square miles of territory along a tortuous 26,000-mile coastline, and keeping expenses as low as possible, meant an endless procession of challenges.

Air service crept up on the steamship passenger trade by degrees. In 1929, newspapers reported as a great feat the first commercial passenger flight from Alaska to San Francisco in one day. In 1940 Pan American started the original air service between Alaska and the Outside with flying boats, then used land planes after the airstrip at Juneau was built. In Juneau it was possible to connect with other airlines, but the feeder lines had a small capacity. Service to coastal towns like Ketchikan and Wrangell was hampered by lack of airfields.

After World War II, four-engine DC-4s were available as Army and Navy surplus and a number of small scheduled and nonscheduled airlines developed. The Army chain of airfields, Annette Island, Cordova, Anchorage, Fairbanks and King Salmon, became available, in addition to the airfield at Juneau.

P.F. Gilmore explained, "The government was giving subsidies to airlines to carry passengers. That was one of our problems when the Alaska Line quit passenger service. Also there was the unwillingness of the unions to adjust to low passenger loads in winter, when we often carried more crew than passengers. As an example of what we were up against, air passage to Seward in 1952 was $105 and ours was $115. The air fare did not cover the actual cost; the government made up the difference."

Many people have said that the coming of planes took something away from Alaskan travel. A resident commented, "It used to be old home week when the boats were in port. People went around renewing acquaintances. Now it's a different type of population; they don't know one another as well as we did."

When canneries were able to avail themselves of air service, there was a large reduction in the travel carried by Alaska Steam. The company changed its policy of protecting space for Alaskans during the summer months, and put on campaigns to extend the tourist season. Summers were still profitable times for carrying passengers, but the ships were operated the year-round. Therefore, what had been a necessary service for travelers, became a losing proposition for the line.

Times were changing for the Alaska Steamship Company. The liners had become decidedly outdated. Frequent complaints were heard from military personnel traveling back and forth that there were no private baths for the majority of passengers, and no play areas for children. When the Federal Maritime Board withdrew charter privileges and subsidy payments from Alaskan carriers, the financial difficulties in chartering privately owned ships forced the company to face the inevitable. The Alaska Line had

been in passenger service 59 years and it was the last of the coastwise lines to succumb to increasing costs. Passenger operations had been at a loss. Although the number of travelers to Alaska was increasing, few of them used ships; most went directly by air.

Alaska Steam announced on July 6, 1954, that it was going out of the passenger business. At the end of August, when the *Alaska* sailed from Kodiak, residents of the island were saddened; they felt that there might no longer be tourists to enliven the little town with their visits.

The final passenger trip was made by the *Denali* in September. Her last visit to Seward was described as "just like attending a funeral." At Valdez people came from miles around to bid her farewell. Some were near tears when strains of "Auld Lang Syne" floated out from the ship as she pulled away from the dock. It was foreseen that the halt to service meant a change in the town's life. Capt. Albert McCabe felt nostalgic himself as he made his adieus; he had first visited Valdez in 1927 as a cabin boy.

The *Denali* was sold to the Peninsular and Occidental Line at the end of the year.

As the company disposed of its passenger liners the *Victoria*, then a freighter, was purchased by Dulien Steel Products in 1954. She was 84 years old.

Another sale in 1954 was the *Aleutian* to the Caribbean Atlantic Line. The last of the passenger fleet to go, in 1955, were the *Alaska*, sold to Margo Pacific Line, and *Baranof*, sold for scrapping in Japan.

And so, a gallant flotilla of passenger vessels disappeared from the Northwest Coast. Life in the little ports of Alaska has not been quite the same since.

C. Form 867.

File No. L 1284

SERIAL NUMBER
140696

ISSUE NUMBER
89

UNITED STATES DEPARTMENT OF COMMERCE
BUREAU OF NAVIGATION AND STEAMBOAT INSPECTION

LICENSE TO MASTER OF STEAM AND MOTOR VESSELS

This is to certify that *John Newland* has given satisfactory evidence to the undersigned United States Local Inspectors, Bureau of Navigation and Steamboat Inspection, for the district of *Seattle, Wash,* that he can safely be intrusted with the duties and responsibilities of Master of Steam and Motor Vessels of not over *any* gross tons, upon the waters of *Oceans: also Pilot on Bay and Harbor of New York, and Southeastern and Southwestern Alaska.*

and is hereby licensed to act as such Master for the term of five years from this date.

Given under our hands this *13th* day of *Jan.*, *1937*

Daniel B. Hutchings.
U.S. Local Inspector of Hulls.

William N. Campbell
U.S. Local Inspector of Boilers.

O Form 1190

Captains and Crew

It takes more than ships to guarantee a shipping firm's success. It takes capable men. Until the advent of modern electronic aids such as loran, radar and depth finders, navigating Alaskan waters was a constant challenge. The men who commanded the Alaska Steamship Company fleet, plying the most hazardous waters in the world, had to be exceptionally capable to survive.

In sixty years of serving the nation's northernmost shores, Alaska Steam lost only eighteen ships to marine casualties, only three of them during World War II.

The following account, taken from the workbook of the late Capt. John Newland, describes some typical, tense hours on the SS *Latouche* in November 1923:

> *Passed out by Cape Spencer at 2 a.m. Nov. 2 and encountered ENE gale and rough sea. Had five cows and one horse as part of deck cargo bound for Anchorage. As the wind was fair and sea in favor, expected to make Cape St. Elias the following morning*

◄**Captain Newland's Master's certificate.**

> *(Nov. 3) about 4:30, being only 264 miles from point to point. I got up at midnight on account of weather being hazy and ship steering badly and walked up and down the bridge, watching out for light on Cape St. Elias.*
>
> *As no light came in sight, at 3 a.m. ordered second officer to take soundings with machine lead on afterdeck. He did so but got no bottom at 3 or 3:30 or 4 a.m. Every minute we were expecting to see the light.*
>
> *At 5:30 a.m. I told him to cast the lead again, which he did. Then he ran to the bridge and reported shoal water. I told him to take another cast and get a true depth. He returned and reported only 28 fathoms.*
>
> *Right away I slowed the engines and swung the ship's head to the east. Called the pilot and other officers to assist me in locating the ship's position. But the farther we steamed . . . the less water we got.*

Capt. John Newland was born in the Baltic state of Latvia. After completing school, including mastery of three languages, he went to sea. His first berth was as cook's helper on a German Baltic schooner. He made voyages around Cape Horn on German square-rigged sailing vessels and was shipwrecked on the coast of northern Scotland. He joined a British bark, the Strathdon, commanded by Captain Philip, one of the rare sailing ship-masters who gave apprentices the seagoing education their parents paid for — and also permitted the seamen to attend classes when they were not on watch.

Newland landed in the United States in the 1890s and attended navigation school in Brooklyn, New York. He was licensed as a pilot for the bay and harbor of New York and sailed on steam-ships to Caribbean ports and to Central and South America.

As a mate on a steamer being delivered to the Alaska Steam-ship Company, he traveled to Seattle via the Strait of Magellan (the Panama Canal had not yet been completed) and found the Puget Sound country so attractive that he bought acreage to make sure he would come back.

Settling his affairs in the East, he returned to Seattle the same year and joined the Alaska Steamship Company, sailing with the pioneer Alaska ship-masters including Capt. John A. O'Brien who was known to newspaper readers as Dynamite Johnny. His first command, which came through a recom-mendation from Captain O'Brien, was the SS Dora, the "Bulldog of Alaska," which sailed from Seward to the Alaska Peninsula and Aleutian Island ports.

Subsequently he commanded ten other Alaska Steamship Com-pany vessels including the SS Victoria. In the mid-'20s, the SS Redondo sailed out of Seward to the Kodiak Island group, serving remote ports and shuttling cargoes to and from the Alaska Steamship Company freighters calling at Seward. It was the first time that a "large" freight steamer had been to some of them. With his officers, Captain Newland charted safe water and obstacles. The findings were reported to the U.S. Coast and Geodetic Survey which put his name on the Shuyak Island cape at the west end of Shuyak Island.

In the late 1920s and early 1930s, he commanded Alaska Steamship Company ships carry-ing freight to Bering Sea ports as far north as Point Barrow.

After 43 years of seafaring, he was forced to leave the sea due to ill health. He died in 1942.

Capt. John Newland

Eventually I came to the conclusion that we had overrun our distance and were under Middleton Island. So I changed course. Then we got in 15 fathoms of water with heavy ground swell. The ship was laboring heavily. Cargo was shifting on deck and in between decks, throwing the cattle around and injuring one.

I decided to put the ship on the old course, to head her back of Middleton Island and get her out of the trough of the sea. Also, we received a radio compass bearing showing that we were right on track. But how could we be there with such a depth of water?

After we had sailed for a couple of hours, we sighted Cape St. Elias, and an hour or so later passed same seven miles off, showing radio compass bearings correct — but sounding on chart incorrect, maybe through earthquake disturbances. Later reported same by wireless to company at Seattle; also to the agents along the line.

The masters, frequently of Scandinavian ancestry, were notable personalities. Many had gone to sea as young men and come up through the ranks of the Alaskan maritime service. Often they were remembered best by their nicknames. When company employees got together they spoke of Dynamite Johnnie O'Brien, Jolly Julius Johansen, Gus Nord or Laughing Jack Johnson.

"In Alaska," said Bob Rose, "we probably had the finest pilots in the world. The difference between an experienced Alaskan pilot and a deep-sea navigator was that the Alaskan was skilled in taking directions from points on the beach."

A mate, F.W. Ross, explained this distinction. "In the days before radar, to maintain the middle of the channel we'd blow the whistle and listen for the echo from surrounding mountains. You ran your ship by timing your speed and your channel lights. We'd average about 12 knots — five minutes to every mile. You sailed the Inside Passage by points instead of degrees. There was one mate who insisted on staying on course within a degree and a half. We nicknamed him 'Small 8' because of that."

Capt. Maurice Reaber described his experience: "I was fortunate to learn my piloting from old-timers on the Inside Passage, beginning in 1921. There were no radar, depth finders, gyroscopic compasses or loran then; in fact we had nothing but the compass, lead line, whistle for echoes, and our own eyes and ears. Navigational aids were not what they are now. In the Aleutians, vast areas never had been surveyed. The charts were sprinkled with P.D. [Position Doubtful] and E.D. [Existence Doubtful]. Whole big spaces were surrounded by dotted lines which marked unsurveyed areas.

"The former bridge log was our bible. The creed was that if the ship had made the course under like conditions in the past, she should be able to make it again. Therefore the bridge officer would always have three logbooks out for flood tide, ebb and slack. All logs were carefully kept: courses, standard compass, steering compass and the time in hours or minutes run. This routine was scrupulously maintained, no matter if the run was in daylight or clear. The mate on watch was the bookkeeper and he looked after the quartermaster. During the night the pilot never looked at a chart course book or anything else; he depended upon the mate to keep time and, when the weather was thick, let him know when to change course. Time, distance and course — you ran full speed as long as you dared, because as soon as you slowed down, time and distance were lost. Then you had to grope your way by whistle echo, or, as we said, 'smell your way.' Little did we imagine that someday there would be a black box to look in and see the shoreline and other ships.

"If a vessel had a tendency to sag to one side the pilot had to see that he steered the other way to average the course. Two drawers in the pilothouse were for the running charts. One chart, showing the water the ship was in, was always on the chart table. When the ship ran out of that chart, a new chart was brought forth and the old one went into the lower drawer. On the return trip, the order was reversed."

Reaber asked an old-time pilot, "How in the world can you remember so many magnetic courses in your head?"

"I see the inside run as a picture in my mind," the veteran replied, "complete with courses and points of change."

It was important, as Captain Reaber said, that a ship maintain the same speed as long as possible, for the moment she slowed, the position was lost. From that point the pilot groped with the whistle for an echo and estimated distances. In winter, with short days and snowstorms, some ships were bound to run aground. In the later years of the company after radar was installed, although bad weather still presented a problem, no ships were lost.

Former mate Ross recalled his most exciting moments on the run. "I was on the *Alaska*, southbound out of Ketchikan," he said, "when we got into a sudden fog. We had only lights to guide us at Herbert Reef near Dixon Entrance. The pilot came onto a reef before he thought we should and up we went. It was at half tide. Everybody got into life jackets, but there was no excitement because there were few passengers. There was no damage to the ship and after several hours we were off the reef at high tide."

Capt. John G. "Gus" Nord, one of the most renowned captains of the line, was noted for having a level head. He remained on the bridge 72 hours at a stretch with no sleep except catnaps. He was born in Sweden and came to Seattle as a young sailor. He quickly acquired mate's papers, and in the third year of being in the country he became a master. A strict disciplinarian, he was much respected by his crew. He lived to the age of 71 and was still a pilot for Alaska Steam when he met a tragic death.

An early story about him was related by Edward (E.P.) Morgan. In October 1918, Captain Nord left Ketchikan for Seattle with a capacity load of 350 first-class and 400 steerage passengers on the *Alaska*. In the cargo were 2,000 tons of sacked copper ore, 30,000 cases of salmon and 200 tons of other goods; among them $2,700,000 in gold bullion, $150,000 worth of furs and $250,000 in currency.

Halfway down the narrows in Finlayson Channel, between Sarah Island and the mainland, the steering gear fractured and the *Alaska* sheered to port. She was caught in a fast incoming tide and her rudder was useless; she was heading straight for a 500-foot bluff. Nord ordered the engines reversed but was too late. The quick-thinking captain gave the astonishing signal for "full speed ahead" and when the ship crashed into the rock, she stayed glued there. It was Nord's idea to see whether he could stop the impending hole in her bow with cargo.

"He held her nose to the bluff for the next 15 minutes," Morgan wrote, "while passengers were taken off. Twelve mental patients grabbed the lowering tackle and dumped a boatload into the sea. All were fished out and the boat was righted. Meanwhile Nord had the crew bring sacks of copper ore from the hold and stack them against the collision bulkhead."

Swanson Bay was the nearest port, but passengers were refused shelter anywhere there except in wharf warehouses, because of some influenza cases aboard ship. The purser's staff took turns through the night guarding the bullion and currency on the dock.

By morning Nord freed the *Alaska* from her rocky perch and brought her into Swanson Bay, but considered the ship's condition too risky to take the passengers on again. He let them aboard for meals during the 36 hours they waited until the *Jefferson* arrived to carry them and the treasure to their destination. A little more than two days later Nord steamed into Seattle, having saved his ship and cargo.

Capt. Maurice Reaber related another story about Nord and a new mate when Nord was captain of the *Northwestern*. To show how efficient he was on the job, the new mate had the gangplank hanging over the side before the ship docked. Meanwhile Nord missed his aim and had to back out and make a round turn with the gangplank hanging over the side. As Reaber put it, "The poor mate caught hell. The embarrassed captain yelled at him to get the gangplank aboard, demanding, 'Are you trying to make a monkey of me?'"

Another of Morgan's anecdotes dated from Nord's assignment to the *Jefferson*. Nord heard the complaint of a big fellow who claimed to have been cheated at gambling on the boat. Nord told the man he was a fool to have let himself get skinned, but having done so it was a childish act to come to the captain about it. "I'd have kicked the head off the guy who was cheating and got my money back," Nord told him. The passenger took the captain's comment to heart. Soon afterward there were sounds of fighting. The victim got back his cash. Nord congratulated him, saying, "If you ever travel with me again, I hope you know enough to keep out of crooked games."

Nord was in command of the *Aleutian* when she fetched up on a reef off Kodiak Island. She sank in less than ten minutes. Although all on board were saved except one, this was an inexplicable accident for a man so skilled and cautious, who in 35 years of sailing had not lost a vessel. Nord's license was suspended for 60 days. He was hurt. He never again took over a ship, but became a pilot on the same run instead. When the vessel he was on docked in Haines, he went for an automobile ride with friends. While they were traveling along a scenic road, the car overturned at the edge of the shore, and Captain Nord was trapped in the rear seat and drowned.

Morgan is one of the few sources of information about the famous Dynamite Johnnie O'Brien. Throughout the years it was part of the passenger business to bring out mental patients bound for a sanatorium in Portland, and federal prisoners sentenced to McNeil Island. About 1910, when O'Brien was on the *Northwestern*, one of the patients got loose, ran into the galley, snatched up a cleaver and rushed out on deck swinging the blade. The man was a husky 200-pounder and those he encountered were terrified. A seaman hastened to tell Captain O'Brien, who was eating his dinner. Excusing himself, the dapper captain went out on deck and approached the madman, who made a couple of swings at him and struck him in the shoulder. Nevertheless the captain succeeded in tripping and disarming the fellow. The weapon clattered on deck and the captain, disregarding his own cuts, sat on the man until he was safely placed in irons and taken away.

Though polite in his language to passengers, O'Brien had a wonderful vocabulary of oaths. Morgan told about one night when women passengers heard him cussing out the mate. Not knowing its source, the next morning they reported the violent outburst to the captain. O'Brien pretended to be shocked and promised there would be no profanity on his ship. "Ladies," he said, "I shall investigate this and when I find the guilty man I will discharge him."

Captain O'Brien was commanding the *Edith* as she wallowed across the Gulf of Alaska. He called down to the engine room for more power.

"You're getting all you're going to get," replied the chief engineer. O'Brien answered, "Take your choice, you old so and so — either give me some more steam or you'll be shoveling coal in hell in less than an hour."

Of Capt. Charles A. Glasscock, one of his officers recalled: "He never drank or smoked. When he was skipper, the passengers had to conform as closely as possible to the rules he set for the crew. Of course he couldn't control drinking in the staterooms, but let anyone wander out on deck drunk, and Captain Glasscock got him under cover at once."

An agent up North told one yarn about Captain Glasscock, when he was crossing Prince William Sound with the *Yukon*, his longtime command. The *Yukon* passed the *Mount McKinley* and paused to transact some company business. During the interval an assistant purser from the *Yukon* jumped aboard the *McKinley* to chat with another officer. When the ships disengaged and went their ways, the visiting purser was still aboard the *Mount McKinley*. The captain notified the *Yukon* by radio, "We've got one of your pursers on board. What should we do with him?"

"Keep the bastard," Captain Glasscock replied promptly.

Captain Glasscock, who used to boast that he was the first white child born on Lopez Island in the San Juans, had sailed for twelve years on the Admiral line before joining Alaska Steam in 1923. He was master of the *Northwestern*, the *Yukon*, the *Victoria* and the *Columbia* at different times, and he received a gold medal for bringing the first steamship to enter port at Petersburg. He retired in 1946 and died in 1951. Devoted as his life had been to the Alaska run, he had asked to have his ashes scattered off Cape St. Elias. The *Denali* performed this service for him.

Capt. Joseph Ramsauer, though he had been an art student, was with Alaska Steam for 41 years. He was captain of the *Nizina* when, in 1930, Capt. Robert Nordstrom was second mate. "That year Jack Sloan was third mate," Nordstrom said, "and Emery Joyce, whose father was a sea captain and who was to become a captain himself, was only a seaman. On April Fool's Day, Joyce decided it would be a good joke to mix soap grease with the butter. Early that morning, Captain Ramsauer sent Jack Sloan down to get him toast and coffee. When the captain bit into the toast he sputtered, and yelled, 'What are you trying to to — poison me?'

" 'Yes, sir, yes, sir,' Sloan stammered. He didn't know what he was being blamed for. A long time afterward Joyce admitted what he had done. He was a kid just out of high school then."

Capt. Raymond Dowling related, "I spent much time with Captain Ramsauer and he was a mighty fine teacher. I learned a lot. He tolerated absolutely no drinking on the ship. If you had a smell of it you were fired. Once we left Seward in a heavy wind and the bonnet on the stack blew loose and rattled. I went up with a line to keep it from blowing overboard. It was bitter cold and I could hardly get down, my hands were so chilled. Ramsauer took me to his room and gave me a shot of booze — that's the only time I ever saw liquor around him."

Ramsauer had only one accident during his many years as captain. Near Smith Island, just after leaving Seattle, he ran onto Hein Bank and tore 17 bottom plates.

Grenville Channel

Seattle to Ketchikan	Port or Starboard Beam	Dist. off. Miles	True Course	Mag. Course	Mag. in Points	Dist. from Pt. to Pt.	Dist. from Point of Departure	Dist. to Destination
Union Pass 	p.b.	¾	**N43W**	**N72W**	W×N⅝N	4.4	506.7	143.4
Lowe Inlet, North Pt. 	s.b.	¼—	"	"	"	9.3	516.0	134.1
Mountain Pt. 	s.b.	⅛	**N39W**	**N68W**	WNW	2.2	518.2	131.9
Bushy Slide	p.b.	⅛	"	"	"	3.2	521.4	128.7
Serpent Waterfall 	p.b.	¼—	**N35W**	**N64W**	NW×W⅝W	0.3	521.7	128.4
Klewnuggit Lt. Favor the West shore passing here. Tides meet here.	s.b.	⅜	"	"	"	3.5	525.2	124.9
Granite Cliff  Put Klewnuggit Lt. astern.	s.b.	½	**N40W**	**N69W**	W×N⅞N	3.3	528.5	121.6

Lowe Inlet.

The ship floated on her tank tops. He had to turn around and head for dry dock, at which point the oil dripped out steadily. A member of the crew said they were mopping black bunker oil off the dry dock for several days.

Reaber told an anecdote about Captain Cochran when he was on the *Victoria*. "One day in Ketchikan we were lying alongside the cold storage dock and it was blowing hard. The captain was an extremely mild-mannered man. Nobody had ever seen him get excited or cuss. A big crowd was on the dock, among them a drunk.

"We had our spring line out and had backed away, but before we could get into the stream we were alongside the city dock right next to the one where we had been. All this time the drunk was shouting instructions as to how we should be handling the ship. We worked with the spring line all over again, but didn't make it. The ship came up alongside the lumber dock, with the drunk following us.

"The *Vic* was long, deep and hard to manage. Captain Cochran was figuring out what to do next when the drunk yelled, 'Captain, you don't know how to handle your ship. Go ahead on your starboard screw and back on your port screw.'

"This was too much for the captain, who shouted, 'You yellow-bellied so and so, as soon as I get the ship tied up I'm going to kick you all the way from here to Front Street.'

"This was great entertainment for the passengers and they cheered, 'You tell 'em, Captain!' The last we saw of the

◄A page from the *Hand Book for Puget Sound, Southeastern and Southwestern Alaska* by S.E. Hansen, master mariner.

drunk, he was squirming out of the crowd as fast as he could go. That line from the captain even quieted the wind. It let up so we had no more trouble and got right out of there."

Capt. Julius Johansen of the *Alameda*, who was very popular with the women passengers, became known as Jolly Julius. Although he danced with the ladies, he would not permit any of his staff to do so.

In the fall of 1918 he was in at Valdez. Because a north wind was blowing he was afraid to anchor, so he kept cruising up and down the harbor. While he was doing so the *Northwestern* came in and tied up without effort. Johansen approached and requested, "Can I tie up beside you?" Captain Jensen laughingly replied, "I'll let you tie up to my ship if you think you can do it."

Nicknames were not confined to captains; there were Dirty Neck Stone (a pilot), Big Andy, Big Jake, and Squeaky Anderson. Squeaky Anderson had a voice like a girl's, but he became famous for his exploits in World War II. Also remembered were Cock-Eyed Anderson; Big Anderson; Gentleman Charlie Davis; and a mate, Russian Finn Kelly, a massive man who would go berserk at the sight of lumber. If the crew didn't move timbers fast enough to suit him he would jump into the hold and lift the timber himself. He managed to ruin his back with such antics over the years. Other Alaska Line regulars with memorable nicknames were Jack "Kidney Foot" Williams, a cook; Capt. "Net-sling" Johnson; Capt. "Magic" Hanson; and Big Jack and Little Jack Dillon. Both of the Dillons were stewards at one time.

A pilot called Chippy Dodge was asked by a woman passenger how he got his peculiar nickname. "I was irresistible," he responded. He was so short, a box was kept in the pilothouse for him to stand on. Another of his contemporaries was Capt. "Speakeasy" Westerhold, who always talked in a low monotone.

Best remembered among pursers was Dave Doran, 32 years on the Alaska Line, who began as a freight clerk in 1919. He retired in 1950. His longest assignment was on the *Alaska*, where he was known to be the special enemy of stowaways. One day freight clerk William Taylor challenged a big Swede at Ketchikan, insisting that he must show his ticket at the gangplank. The fellow pushed past him and headed for the steerage. Taylor notified Doran, his boss. Dave put on his cap and coat, saying sarcastically, "Oh, so he wouldn't show his ticket!" He disappeared in the direction of the steerage. When he returned to his office he was a sight to behold, his jacket torn, one sleeve out, his glasses broken and tie hanging loose.

"You're right," he told Taylor. "He wouldn't show his ticket."

Taylor remembered another incident when he was Doran's assistant. Tom Healy, chief officer, was a great hand for pawing through Doran's papers, so one night Dave decided to get even. He faked a telegram reading, "Understand one of your crew has illicit game meat aboard. Impound this for one of our officers to board you." He signed it with the name of Frank Dufresne, head of the Alaska Game Department.

Healy entered, thumbed through the purser's papers as usual, found this wireless and read it. He turned crimson and darted out, the purser's staff could guess what for.

"We were all out there to greet him when he appeared with a bundle of meat," Taylor said. "We gave him a big hoorah and he knew then he'd been jobbed."

Another purser, Bill Hickman, held a record for being where the wrecks were. On his first trip in 1929 he was on the original *Aleutian* when she hit the reef and sank at Amook Bay, Kodiak Island. He was on the *Columbia* when she ran aground at Pulley Point near Alert Bay in a dense fog. While he was on the *Northwestern* she struck a reef across from Sentinel Island. The lifeboats were lowered, but it was discovered there was no imminent danger so the passengers were taken back aboard. The ship ran for the sandy mouth of Eagle River, where she was beached and all could walk ashore. Hickman was chief purser on the *Yukon* in 1946 when she broke her back 40 miles east of Seward. He was also aboard the *Mount McKinley* in an Aleutian convoy when she crashed near Scotch Cap, a total loss.

Endless anecdotes are told about the characters associated with the Alaska Line through the years. For instance, Ned Skinner told about a pilot named Cornell on the *Alaska* who enjoyed feeding the rats that often plagued the vessels. He'd bring them handfuls of cheese and make pets of them. That was about 1925. In later years such a thing would have been impossible; each ship had to qualify for a "deratization" certificate semiannually.

Another well-earned sobriquet was attached to a mate named Peterson on the *Latouche*. The crew dubbed him Barefoot Peter because he used to go out on deck in his bathrobe, barefooted, gnawing a rib bone he'd picked up from the galley.

Ask any former employee what was his most exciting experience on the Alaska run and you get a tale of peril on the high seas. Capt. Adolf Danielson recalled, "Once on the *Depere*, when I was on my first trip as skipper, I got stuck in the ice. We were caught 24 hours. I can tell you it feels terrible to be in ice. I had to leave part of the Nome cargo on the ship. That was hard because the people needed it, but there was no choice. The ice was coming in and we barely managed to get out."

On another voyage during World War II, Captain Danielson was sailing in a convoy when he ran aground in the Shumagin Islands and was an hour and twenty minutes getting off. The convoy went on without him. Another time he got stuck in the ice in the Bering Sea. "That was when my hair turned white," he said. "That voyage was my closest brush with disaster in 46 years on the sea."

Captain Danielson was with Alaska Steam for 38 years and at one time commanded the little *Redondo*. On the westward run his boat was often iced down and he'd have his crew out chopping away at the ice, or going after frozen pipes with a blowtorch. He called at strange places, once at Gambell on St. Lawrence Island, and another time to land oil-drilling equipment at Kanatak. In emergencies he had to make the best of things. On the *Cordova* when he was master, an Eskimo woman once gave birth. Another time, out in the Gulf of Alaska, a man took a drug overdose and left a suicide letter for his wife. "We tried to revive him. We kept busy calling doctors on the radio for advice," Danielson said.

Once in the 1930s the *Depere* sailed through floating lava from an eruption of Mount Pavlof. The air was full of ash and it was like running through a fog.

Observed F.W. "Bill" Ross who was 40 years on the line beginning in 1931:

About as strange as anything that ever happened to me, was an incident on the first trip I made as an ordinary seaman on the Yukon. I didn't know about the custom of having U.S. marshals bring out mental patients for Morningside Hospital [in Oregon]. I'd seen some poor woman sitting and crying, but I didn't know what it was about. The Yukon had a special room for violent patients. It had a barred porthole and hatch. One day as I walked by this hatch, a hand reached out and grabbed me by the ankle. I was so startled I nearly jumped overboard. I looked down and there was a fellow standing on something in the room below. He could reach through the bars and grab anyone passing. That's when I learned about the mental patients we often carried.

I was boatswain on the Alaska when one of the steerage passengers jumped overboard at 2 a.m. in Seymour Narrows. The tide was nine or ten knots and when we went after the fellow in a small boat, we had to go through an overfall. The ship put a floodlight on the guy to guide us. We picked him up near Cape

Mudge, but we traveled ten miles in the boat before the ship could take us aboard.

That reminds me of the time we were at Port Graham, a cannery stop on Cook Inlet. We were discharging cargo when a cannery tender tied up alongside. I was on deck supervising hatches when I noticed a sailor off the tender. He was reeling around, very drunk, trying to get back aboard his boat. Suddenly I heard bullets, and screams from the dock. I looked over the rail and there was this sailor, jug in one hand and revolver in the other. He'd gone berserk and didn't know what he was doing. He tumbled overboard, still hanging onto the bottle. He couldn't swim, but the tide brought him up. We threw life rings at him and got one around his neck. He was pulled aboard the tender. Her captain came on deck, about as drunk as the sailor, and began kicking him around.

Talk about contrasts — you saw plenty on the Alaska run. The cruises attracted many school-teachers. They came aboard with fancy dinner clothes, looking for romance. They outnumbered the male passengers and we'd see the women having to dance with each other.

"Then, every Alaskan town had its red-light district. It wasn't unusual to see a madam coming aboard to say good-bye to one of her girls who was going to try her luck at some other location. They were well-behaved and we seldom heard of their bothering anyone.

Capt. Roy Selig offered another view. "Women tourists seemed more often on the make than the regular red-light ladies, who were very proper because they didn't want people to know what they were. But I remember one prostitute going north on the *Aleutian* who was a rough customer. She walked across the dining room carrying a plate of spaghetti and meat balls, dumped the lot on a passenger's head, and declared, "That's for not paying me."

The Seattle office was not without a few contacts with one of the oldest professions. Bob Rose recalled:

> Two prostitutes had set themselves up in business on a little island in Dutch Harbor, calling their place Pleasure Island. I was on the passenger desk when a blowzy, bossy woman announced herself as Mrs. Brown and said she had discovered a setup out there where two old women "were robbing those nice boys." Mrs. Brown wanted to send her girls up there to furnish some competition on the island. The captain on the Navy station would not let them ashore. Now she was asking Alaska Steam to arrange it so they could land. I wanted to get rid of Mrs. Brown, so I took her in to see my boss. She didn't get any further with her proposition. When she had gone my boss came out and said he didn't want to see any more like her.

> One man from Seward got sick and had no one to care for him, until a prostitute befriended him and nursed him back to health. Time went on and the prostitute was dying of cancer. Her doctor sent her Outside to go to a hospital for treatment, but she had to have someone along to take care of her before we could give her passage. The man decided to return her favor and go with her. Well, he got her as far as Ketchikan. They had to take her off the ship and she died there.

> The man didn't want anything for his services. But when the woman's family, who had rejected her all those years, suddenly became interested in her estate, he came in and said, "All right, I want complete reimbursement of my entire expenses for the trip."

Rose contributed an anecdote about the mental patients:

> Usually they were assembled in parties of ten to twenty when they were sent Outside. The customary arrangement was for a bus to meet them in Seattle.

> One morning, a skipper called me to say there was a woman on board giving birth to a baby. "She's one of the patients from Petersburg," he explained.

> The ship was already entering the harbor when I phoned the Marine Hospital. They refused to receive the woman. I called

Harborview, the county hospital, and was told that if they took her the company must provide a guard. I asked for the boss and finally convinced him they could handle her without a custodian. She and the baby were carried off on a stretcher. As she went she announced that she was going to name the baby Bob, for me.

The hospital wanted a copy of the baby's birth certificate. I said I would get a certified copy of the ship's log, but the folks in the hospital office had never heard of such a thing. By the time we had the matter straightened out the woman had changed her mind and named the baby Baranof, for the boat.

During the war, steamship agents were required to obtain the real names of all the passengers. A certain traveler from a red-light district protested, but the agent stuck with his orders and refused to list her professional name. Then on the way out the *Alaska* ran aground on Graham Reef, in Canadian waters. The woman was thankful she wasn't sailing under a false name. She would have been in trouble with the Canadian authorities, but for the agent's insistence.

As a shoreside agent, John E. Coulter knew many of the ships' personnel. Capt. "Blackie" Selig was a good artist, he recalled, and he painted some excellent pictures of ships and Alaska scenery. "A specialty of his was painting little Christmas scenes around the company emblem on the return address of business envelopes. They were very clever.

"One season Selig made all sorts of kites and sailed them from the ship's decks. Some were so small they were made with soda straws, others quite large.

"Once he got a steam locomotive whistle from the Alaska Railroad in Seward, and mounted it on the *Iliamna*. For several trips, Alaska ports heard the strange sound of a railroad whistle announcing the arrival of a steamship. The company officials in Seattle took a dim view of this novelty, so before long the *Iliamna* was back to using the whistle she had inherited from the old *Victoria*, the deepest-toned whistle on the coast."

Coulter, who started with the company in Ketchikan in 1952, told of building a dummy bear gun eight feet long. "Tourists off the ships had great fun with it, posing and clowning with this Alaskan-sized weapon," he said. "Now it is in a museum in Valdez, where I moved as agent in 1957."

Coulter served as agent in Bethel and in Sitka, then retired in 1972. His wife, Eula, was one of the last passengers out of Alaska on the Alaska Line. She boarded the southbound *Denali* at Ketchikan in October 1954.

F.W. Ross recalls:
The line used to have a shuttle ship at Cordova. I was on the Latouche when we went in at the herring packing plant near Cordova one Fourth of July. Nobody was on the dock to take our line. We could hear accordions playing in the loft, and a lot of other noise. We blew the whistle, but nobody heard it because of the stomping, dancing and singing. The tide was in and the skipper was afraid to maneuver close enough to the dock so someone could jump ashore.

While he was deciding what to do, two women herring chokers came out, looking bleary-eyed. They signaled they would take the line. A crowd was at the windows of the plant watching, but none came down and helped. But those two drunk dames managed to moor us all right.

Another time, on the Mount McKinley in Icy Strait we saw a 35-foot boat sending up clouds of smoke, and a man and a boy in an outboard, circling her. We got on the windward side and put the fire out, but nearly waterlogged the boat. The man in the outboard said she belonged to a fox farmer who had been picking up salmon heads at a cannery for fox feed.

We sent a sailor down to see what had gone wrong on the burned boat, and he found a dead man lying over the engine. Apparently he had been drunk. The outboard fisherman came alongside and said he would take the body back to Juneau. We wrapped the corpse in a canvas cargo cover. It was badly burned and some of our passengers got sick watching. The chief steward said very few wanted dinner that night. On our homeward-bound trip we stopped at Juneau and picked up the canvas cargo cover. Nobody ever figured what had started the fire,

*but it had pretty well cooked the
boat owner.*

At least two masters of Alaska liners
died at their posts. Capt. Jeremiah Flynn
died of a heart attack aboard the *Redondo*
and his first officer had to take over. Capt.
Rudolph Hanson sailed out of Seattle as
pilot on the *Alaska* on his final voyage. At
Skagway the skipper received word of his
wife's death and had to hurry home.
Hanson took his place as master, but
when the ship was 95 miles from
Petersburg, a heart attack killed him. He
had been with the company for 36 years.

It is said of Capt. Jock Sutherland that
he could smell the obstacles in his course.
A mate who sailed with him never forgot
one foggy night in southeastern Alaska,
when Captain Sutherland startled him
with the order, "Full speed astern."
Shortly afterward the fog lifted, and sure
enough, they had just missed the rocks.
The captain's judgment was unerring.

Will there ever again be captains like
these men who skippered the Alaska
ships before the days of radar? They seem
a vanished breed.

SS *Chena* with her decks piled high with containers.
Puget Sound Maritime Historical Society

CHAPTER 11

The End of the Line

When the Alaska Line became strictly a cargo carrier, emphasis was placed on increasing efficiency. The holds of vessels were paved for smooth movement of forklifts, new masts and extra booms were installed to lift huge vans, pilothouses were raised so pilots could see over vans stacked high on deck, and new generators were installed to provide power for van refrigeration and heat. Such improvements were expensive; a forklift alone cost $34,000 in 1960.

For the first few years the van service was geared to fast transport of military cargo. By 1957 Alaska Steam was recognized as having one of the most highly containerized operations under the American flag. Two vessels sailed each week for southwestern Alaska and one a week for southeastern. Expenses per ton of cargo were showing a downward trend.

The next big development was a 40-foot controlled-temperature trailer van carried on deck. This was a joint effort with the Alaska Railroad. In the end the vans were standardized at 24 by 8 by 8 feet.

Problems of temperature control were worked out so salad greens loaded in Seattle were fresh at the end of the trip. In February 1961, the first such service to Juneau and Ketchikan began with groceries, fresh milk and meat. The vans returned with frozen fish. Anchorage and Fairbanks already were getting similar service. With southbound cargoes of fish there was again an inducement to call at Bellingham, where large orders of fish-trap wire and pilings had been picked up before.

Many cumbersome shipments were carried that year. In May the *Susitna* delivered an entire bank to Bethel. It was a trailer building complete with safes and safety deposit boxes. The *Talkeetna* sailed in June with the largest load of fishing boats ever taken to Alaska; 99 gill-netters, each 32 feet in length, 65 of them were on deck, some hanging over the sides of the ship. That August the *Talkeetna* brought back 323,728 cases of Bristol Bay salmon valued at $11,800,000, a record for one shipload. A shipment from Lynn Canal included an old locomotive on its way to a Tennessee purchaser. It had belonged to the White Pass and Yukon Railroad, which had changed to new diesel engines.

Five Liberty-type vessels acquired by Alaska Steam were modified for containers: the *Chena, Iliamna, Nadina, Fortuna* and *Tonsina*. The *Nadina* and *Tonsina* were nicknamed "the lollipops" because the cells that received the containers had circular pads on top. Otherwise they had no gear whatever. The other three ships had the mechanisms to lift boxes off.

These ships had all been given new names. *Tonsina* was suggested in 1954 by Anchorage schoolchildren; she had been the *Sea Coronet*. The *Chena* had been the *Chief Washakie;* the *Nadina*, the *Dorian Prince*. The *Iliamna* was the former *Edmond Mallet* and the *Fortuna* was the *Volunteer State*. Other vessels acquired about this time were the CI-M-AV1 *Levers Bend*, renamed *Galena;* the *Square Sinnet*, renamed *Tatalina;* and the *Square Knot*, which became the *Tanana*.

The Liberty ships were too large to get into many ports so the CI-M-AV1s took over where they could not go. In 1959, 23 ports of this type in southeastern Alaska were served with 352 calls. They were places where both water depth and maneuvering area were restricted and ships had to pass through hazardous narrows and strong tides. A 1961 company advertisement called attention to the scope of the company service. "Look where we've been — Kake, Orca, Nome, Sitka, Kenai, Alitak, Teller, Valdez, Nome, Homer, Bethel, Haines, Juneau, Kodiak, Uganik, Naknek, Seward, Jap Bay, Pelican, Chignik, Tenakee, Yakutat,

Cordova, Skagway, Klawock, Ouzinkie, Seldovia, Whittier, Auke Bay, Kotzebue, False Pass, Metlakatla, Hawk Inlet, Larsen Bay, Sand Point, Unalakleet, Petersburg, Ward Cove, St. Michael, Port Bailey, Womens Bay, Port Ashton, Port Moller, George Inlet, Captains Bay, Dutch Harbor, Goodnews Bay, Squaw Harbor, Letnikof Cove, Port San Juan, Port Williams, Mount Edgecumbe, Port Wakefield, Port Clarence, Shearwater Bay, Tongass Harbor, Excursion Inlet." In earlier years the routes to some of these places had claimed a heavy toll of ship disasters, but now the ships were radar-equipped and skippers no longer had to guess their way by whistle echoes.

There were other difficulties. Fishing had fallen off and canneries could not calculate accurately how many cans and cartons and how much salt to order in advance. If they did not order in sufficient quantities, it was up to the steamship line to meet the emergency with quick deliveries. Then when the season ended, ships again had to be in readiness because the only workers available to load the canned salmon packs were cannery helpers. They were expected to fly out quickly because of the per diem costs of keeping them beyond the time when they were fully employed.

Changes occurred in the ports themselves. At Whittier the terminal was destroyed by fire in 1953. At Nome the population diminished until the city was almost reduced to a Native town. Calls still had to be made at Kotzebue, usually after June to avoid running into ice. Then the ship might anchor 14 miles offshore, where lighterage would become difficult if the wind arose, slamming the barges

against the ship. In shallow water, ground swell was another complication.

No docks existed on Bristol Bay. The steamers had to anchor out and lighter cargoes. Stevedores had to be brought aboard, fed and lodged for three to five days at a time. Capt. Erling Brastad said 30 to 50 Eskimo and Indian workers lived in the No. 3 hold and slept on folding cots on the *Iliamna*.

Stories were told about the *Chena* at Adak in the Aleutians. The ship was tossed about so much in a gale that the prop came out of the water. Once the wind blew 120 miles per hour, ripping away part of the stack. Captain Brastad related how the wind whistled down and blew fire out of the inspection holes in the boiler fire-boxes. A six-foot tongue of fire shot out at an oiler's rear, and he ran, fanning his smoking hip pockets, while the rest of the engine crew laughed.

Captain Brastad said the men on the freighter *Chena* kept up the tradition of the Christmas ship for several years, taking care of the children in the Jesse Lee Home in Seward. They asked the youngsters to write to Santa Claus, and then picked up the letters. By December they had accumulated between $1,500 and $2,000 worth of gifts such as new clothing, fishing gear, portable radios, guitars and other requested items. They wrapped them in fancy paper and distributed them from the ship according to the old custom.

Capt. Adolf Danielson had a clipping about the trip he made as master of the *Coastal Monarch* in 1953, carrying the

The port of Valdez. The *Chena* is tied up ▶ at left.
Mac's Photo Service

year's supply of groceries, coal and clothing for Kotzebue, Candle, Kiwalik, Kobuk, Deering, Kiana, Noorvik and Selawik. Some of these shipments went to upriver villages by lighter. Danielson became weary of the long waits while the barges handled the unloading. The Eskimos would quit work and the *Coastal Monarch* would lie off a village for a couple of days until they decided to return. The cargo on that season's voyage included a carload of canned milk, a carload of flour, 350 tons of coal in sacks, dredging machinery, 30 tons of dynamite, a carload of cement, 300 tons of petroleum, grease and lubricating oil, and 300 tons of stove and diesel oil.

Virgil Crabb, the last company manager, recalled the great assortment of cargoes he had seen moved by the line in its final years. He said, "We had portable stalls for horses and great stainless-steel thermos bottles 24 feet long for carrying milk. We used to carry moose meat for hunters and live reindeer. We took cattle to Kodiak Island. The worst cargoes were green hides — moose and bear. You opened a van and gagged if they hadn't been salted properly. We hauled skins down for stuffing. We even took the early airplanes up, crated, to be assembled at their destinations. Everything for transportation, including railroad cars, went by way of the Alaska Line in the old days."

Capt. Ludwig Jacobson added to this list one of his oddest deliveries, the first live musk-oxen, from Greenland, destined for Nunivak Island, which he took there aboard the *Lucidor*.

Bob Rose observed, "Almost nothing a consumer uses was produced in the North, but we did try to please Matanuska growers by bringing out some frozen peas for them. They cost more to produce than merchants in the States could sell them for. Everything required by a modern society was shipped north. Our average bill of lading covered 1.3 tons of cargo, which meant a mass of small shipments and lots of paperwork."

The battle over freight rates was resumed when, to meet rising costs, the company put a 10 percent increase into effect on Jan. 1, 1960. The conflict was not resolved until April 1962, when the Federal Maritime Commission decided the charges were justified. One of the allegations by Governor Gruening was that members of the Skinner family made large personal profits, financed directly or indirectly by the people of Alaska.

D.E. Skinner retorted that "any nut who wanted to go into the Alaska water transport business" would have to consider five obstacles, namely: Alaska common carriers operated on less than a ton of cargo per mile; it was mostly a one-way haul, with ships largely southbound in ballast; there was little need for service from November through March; a company had to choose which of 92 ports it would serve; and the populous rail belt section required insulated equipment to maintain 33 to 34 degrees, while outside temperatures ranged from 100 degrees in summer to 60 below in winter.

Without the raise in freight rates, Skinner said, the company would have suffered serious losses. He called Governor Gruening's charges hocus-pocus based on fictitious formulas.

The *Juneau Daily Empire* defended the higher freight rates in an editorial, calling attention also to the irregular competition from increasingly numerous barges and small boats that were entering the picture. It mentioned the large numbers of ships that had been damaged or lost in the Alaska trade and concluded, "We must live with realities, not with daydreams."

In 1963 the company was operating fourteen ships, seven of them year-round. Nearly a decade had passed since the end of passenger service. There was one sailing a week to southeastern Alaska, two sailings to southwestern Alaska connecting with the rail belt, one sailing every three weeks to Kodiak and Cook Inlet, and one every two weeks to Kodiak and Adak.

A note in the spring of 1964 describes the trial of the *Nenana*. She hit ice in the Bering Sea on the first voyage of the year to Nome. Capt. Chris Trondsen was still 200 miles from Nome when an unusually heavy ice pack held him off, so he lay at its edge awaiting developments. He lay out there from June 2 to June 14 when he radioed, "What a frustrating way to run a steamship company!" Aircraft were chartered to look for a lead through the ice, because the people of Nome would soon be out of supplies. A lead was found, but by the time the *Nenana* reached the Nome roadstead she had suffered such a battering she needed repairs.

When she got back to Seattle after three weeks in the ice, she had a 30-foot gash in her port bow and she required 43 new frames and 21 plates. She spent 15 days in dry dock, and her repair bill was nearly five times the original capitalization of Alaska Steam. Add to that the cost of the 20-day delay off Nome and damage to her cargo. The total cost reached nearly $250,000.

Modernization did not prevent accidents from happening. Captain Brastad described the time in 1962 when, during a bad blow on the Gulf of Alaska, the *Chena* lost her propeller near Middleton Island.

"The tug *Wanda* went from Seward and towed her in, with the Coast Guard cutter *Storis* standing by. The weather had calmed and we got into Seward all right, then started back to Seattle in tow by the *Adeline Foss*. Once again we hit bad weather, with winds up to 80 knots. We were 11 days in tow. The towboat had to go at reduced speed during the storm on the gulf, yet the *Chena* had to keep moving steadily. We put one of our anchors on board the tug in Seward and they towed us by our anchor chain. The 40 men on the *Chena* were so grateful to get in safely that they took up a purse for the 12 men on the *Adeline*. The manager of the tugboat company said it was the only time he ever knew that to happen."

The most extraordinary incident in the history of the Alaska Steamship Company vessels was the experience of the *Chena* on Good Friday, March 27, 1964. She was a 10,815-ton Liberty ship. It was Capt. Merrill D. Stewart's first trip as her master. She was lying at the wharf in Valdez in the late afternoon, discharging cargo, and the captain and pilot were having dinner. Suddenly the ship began to tremble violently. The two men rushed up the three companionways to the bridge, to find they were in the midst of a terrible earthquake. Water was coming from all directions. The dock and warehouse had disappeared. The ship was lying over to port. She was raised about 30 feet on a wave and spectators later

swore they could see completely under the 440-foot ship. She heeled to port again, about 50 degrees, and slammed down heavily where the docks had been. Then she made a roll back to starboard, came upright, and rolled heavily again to port.

Stewart could see that she was inside where the small-boat harbor had been, and that there was no water under her. Her bottom was in sight all around and the stern was sitting on broken pilings, rocks and mud.

The ship's log shows that within a minute the lifeboat-stations signal had been sounded. The captain signaled for slow ahead on the engines, then half ahead, and miraculously in about four minutes the *Chena* was moving again. People on shore said she slid sideways off a mat of willows placed as fill in the harbor. She could not turn, but continued along shore with her stern in the mud. Then a big gush of water came off the beach, hit the bow, and swung the ship about 10 degrees. The *Chena* broke free, pushing through the wreckage of a cannery and into the bay. The captain did not expect her to stay afloat in deep water and was prepared to take everyone off in lifeboats. He still had stevedores aboard. Two men had been killed and one injured by the shifting of cargo in the No. 3 hold. The crew behaved extremely well and there was no panic.

D.E. Skinner told about the *Chena*'s ordeal. "This 10,000-ton ship was rolled back and forth on the beach at Valdez, where a moment before stood the dock to which she was discharging cargo. Throughout all this one of the mess men, Fred Numair, hung on with one hand and

operated his movie camera with the other, getting the only known live pictures of the earthquake action. You've heard the phrase 'iron men and wooden ships,' which I'd be the last to dispute. Here was a case of iron men and an iron ship and, fortunately, they both came through."

Before the ship left Valdez the waterfront was afire. The *Chena*'s condensers were plugged with mud and pieces of the dock, so it was necessary for her to stop and anchor half a mile off Valdez. A doctor and nurse were brought aboard to attend the injured man and the dead were sent ashore. Ralph Thompson, one of the officers, went into shock soon after the quake and died of heart failure the next morning.

The ship was not taking water so she proceeded to Cordova, arriving there at seven o'clock the next morning. The injured man was sent by airplane to a Seattle hospital. Divers examined the hull and found only a few dents in it and some nicks in the propeller. Before going south the *Chena* unloaded the rest of her Valdez shipments at Cordova. They were barged back to Valdez and landed on the beach.

Sid Hayman said, "We were lucky we had no ships at Seward or Kodiak during the quake. I went up on Sunday to see what we could do. The *Tonsina*, on her maiden voyage as a van ship, had been headed for Seward, but the earthquake had knocked out the cranes on the dock and she could not work. She was due in Monday, but she went on to Anchorage, the first boat in there that season. The Coast Guard cutter *Storis* went ahead of her to break the ice. I went to Anchorage. Things were so bad in the town that our agent did not know he had a ship in.

◀ **BARRACKS IN ALASKA** — This famous Bruckner Building — literally an entire community under one roof — provides every accommodation for 1,700 to 3,000 single servicemen and officers at the Army port of Whittier, Alaska. To save both money and space, every facility is concentrated in the seven stories of steel and concrete — living quarters, mess halls, clubs, theater, hospital, library, hobby shops, PX, snack bars, bank, post office, gym, training rooms, photo lab, rifle range, reception and recreation rooms, barber and beauty shops. This famous composite building, together with the Hodge apartment building for servicemen's families, are reportedly the two largest buildings built under supervision of the Corps of Engineers since the Pentagon. The $4,000,000 Hodge apartment building — housing 177 servicemen's families — and the $6,500,000 Bruckner Building, rise spectacularly in the narrow space between the ice-free hidden harbor and the glacier-cut mountains which rise precipitously from the sea. Combating tremendous winter snowfalls and excessive summer rains, they are connected with heated, lighted tunnels. The two amazing structures actually made Whittier a completely modern city of two buildings. The Bruckner Building was turned over by the Corps of Engineers to the U.S. Army three years ago. Prime contractors were Haddock Engineers Ltd. & Associates of Oceanside, California. Servicemen, duties and desires permitting, could spend an entire tour of duty in this one great building. (Press release, circa 1945, from Alaska District, Corps of Engineers, U.S. Army, Anchorage.)

U.S. Army photo

There were no communications. National Guardsmen were all over, keeping people out of the business district because of ruptured gas mains. The first obstacle we met when we tried to go to the dock was an Eskimo with a bayonet. We got the ship in, with a lot of cooperation, and the Civil Air Patrol flew the cargo to Seward. We had no receipts or papers, but we got the cargo delivered."

Bill Cruchon, radio operator on the *Iliamna,* described his experience. "We were just in from the run to Seward. We arrived in Seattle that night. My nine-year-old son had a little radio. He came into our bedroom and told me there had been a quake at Seward. It didn't register with me — I wanted to go to sleep. He came back a little later and said everything was wrecked at Seward. That finally registered and alerted me so we turned on the TV. After the quake our ship laid up in Seattle for ten days and left with a much bigger deckload than normal, all hand-stowed. We took it to Whittier, but couldn't unload there. The railroad tracks were underwater and the train couldn't get in, so we went to Anchorage. That was the first time I'd ever been there. The dock was usable and we were able to take all the cargo off."

The earthquake thrust the town of Whittier into prominence as a roll-on, roll-off port. The Army had constructed wilderness castles there: the $8,000,000 Bruckner Building and the 14-story apartment tower called the Hodge Building. It was easy to make quick repairs there and the port thrived; by 1967 it was unloading more than 227,000 tons of freight from the Alaska Line.

Ice never ceased to be an obstacle on the Bering Sea. In 1964 the *Tanana* and *Coastal Monarch* were prevented from delivering cargo to Bethel on the Kuskokwim. The ships had to drop anchor 45 miles from port. Later that same year, in September, the *Nenana* raced the ice pack to get freight ashore at the mouths of rivers before they were clogged. She carried groceries, half a dozen freezer vans of perishables, two trailer houses, petroleum, construction materials for a new vocational school at Nome, a new sawmill for Alakanuk up the Yukon, and cans and cartons for next year's salmon pack.

The last ship the Alaska Steamship Co. lost was the *Oduna,* which was stranded in heavy seas on the east side of Unimak Island Nov. 26, 1965. The ship's radar was inoperative and the current must have carried her onto the rocks. The chief mate, on the bridge at the time, was later held to blame and suspended. The crew was removed by helicopter and breeches buoy to the Coast Guard cutter *Storis* and the tug *Adeline Foss.* At first the wreck appeared to be a total loss, but three men organized an effort to remove the cargo, including 200,000 pounds of frozen crab in refrigerated vans. The crab meat and much other cargo and gear were saved.

The Alaska Steamship Company did not make news very often after that. In 1965 and 1966 it was losing money, while company officials endeavored to find a remedy. The year of the earthquake had been a difficult one with the destruction of ports, the near-record late breakup of the ice in Bering Sea, the costly damage to the *Nenana,* the heavy southeastern Alaska salmon run and the firm's inability to charter extra ships.

A group of New York management consultants was called in. The operation was thoroughly investigated and reorganization begun. New departments and new positions were created, but it seemed to old employees that an atmosphere of confusion prevailed.

As one of them observed, "We were stuck with slow Liberty ships. We should have changed back in the 1950s to more efficient vessels. But even had we done so, I don't think it is in the cards for a company to make money in the Alaska trade — certainly not for the type of operation in which we prided ourselves, like running ten hours up to Haines, where there was not enough cargo to pay for the trip. We went everywhere ships were wanted, and you can't do that. We couldn't afford to have all the vans we needed, nor all the trucks. To have the right equipment in the right place cost a lot of money."

The company had made one striking effort to modernize in 1963 when it purchased the Japanese-built *City of New Orleans,* a modern train ship, but she could not operate out of Puget Sound because the Jones Act barred vessels constructed abroad from trade between U.S. ports, so the company based the train ship at New Westminster, British Columbia, under a separate corporation. She could carry 56 rail cars. She also became the third vessel to bear the name *Alaska.* The Seattle firm operated her until December 1974 and made 500 round-trips with her to Whittier. She had American officers and a Canadian crew, and she sailed under the Liberian flag. Capt. Erling Brastad was her skipper until the Skinner corporation sold her to the

Crowley Maritime Corp. By then Crowley had become one of the old line's main competitors.

Another catastrophe affected Alaska Steam adversely in its final years; the fire in Cordova on April 4, 1968. Before the earthquake the company had dredged there to provide a minimum depth of 20 feet at its dock. Though service was reduced after the closing of the Kennecott mine, ships of the line still called at Cordova regularly every two weeks. This dock represented the beginning of the town; it was the original dock, 600 feet long and 90 feet wide. The earthquake raised land in the harbor seven feet. No additional dredging could be done because the piling would have no penetration. Although conditions were not so good as before, the canneries still made Cordova an important port.

By 1968 the company had shifted heavily to containers. There was no point in running the *Tonsina* and the *Nadina* to Cordova because they were dependent upon shore cranes. Now the dock was not strong enough to hold a crane. One was installed by the stevedore firm at Valdez, because Alaska Steam had been putting vans from other ships ashore at this port.

Fifteen or twenty container-loads of canned salmon were waiting at Cordova to be moved to Seattle early in the year. Bob Rose explained, "By then the state ferries were running and I figured at first we could take the vans by ferry to Valdez, but ICC regulations prevented this. So instead we installed a pad, a strong section of dock on which we could set a crane. We brought one from Valdez, just got it all set to go, when the dock caught fire."

A contractor was repairing the planking; employees were using acetylene torches for cutting heads off bolts on the bull rail (the timbers around the edge of the dock). The Standard Oil Company had a pipeline from where the tankers pumped out oil to storage tanks on a nearby hill. The pit at the dock end of the pipeline was oil-soaked. A spark from a torch fell down into the pit and immediately blazed up. The entire dock burned in four hours. With it went 30 to 40 containers, the crane and the Parks cannery. This calamity ended Cordova's life as a port.

The Alaska Line put the vans on the ferry and brought them to the town's tiny dock at the boat harbor. This went on for several months at a financial loss, with the company carrying the burden to serve the community which had so long been its key loading place. Then the firm hired a contractor to rebuild a small section of the old dock for a crane pad. It installed a new crane, almost as big as the structure that held it, and an approach was built so truckers could come down for loads. A ship had to tie to dolphins on either side, and a catwalk was built over a burned section of dock so the vessel's lines could be taken and tied to remaining pilings.

"The fire," Bob Rose continued, "was a disaster for us. There were three canneries in Cordova. We'd just got our van ships and had all that salmon waiting to move on our line. We had plans to pick up empty vans at Seward and take them to Cordova, but now, with Cordova out, the van ships ran full northbound and empty southbound. That was an absolute killer.

"Then Sealand came along, competing

with us. We had a lot of loyal customers, but not enough. Most of the docks were inefficient so we had gone to a barge service ourselves. A barge can land on just a piece of level ground.

"Our Liberty ships, which moved at 10 knots, had crews of 39 each. The maintenance of a ship is an expensive thing. We were competing with tugs and barges with seven-man crews, carrying about the same cargo. Sealand could go twice as fast as we could. We were still stuck with 10 knots."

There may have been some hope with the sailing of Barge 275 for southeastern Alaska in March 1968. This craft was intended to inaugurate full container-ship service and replace two conventional vessels. But skyrocketing inflation, high labor costs and maintenance, new competitive automated containers, sea trains, petroleum and breakbulk barges, combined with airline mail service and foreign money competition, took their toll of the Alaska Steamship Company. By the winter of 1970, operations were reduced to two ships serving Kodiak, Adak and a few small intermediate ports.

The company ran barges for eight months, but could no longer struggle against the overwhelming odds. On Jan. 16, 1971, the Alaska Steamship Company announced that it was going out of business because of insufficient revenue to meet rapidly increasing expenditures. The last ship to sail was the *Fortuna,* on Jan. 29. The company still owned the *Chena, Iliamna, Nenana, Tatalina* and *Polar Pioneer.* In less than two years, all were sold. The *Iliamna* went to a Far East scrap heap. The last to go, in 1972, was the *Polar Pioneer,* which became a mother ship in the tuna fishery. The company had done everything possible to cut down the cost of handling individual cargoes, but was, as one employee said, "still trying to be too nice to the trade."

Much nostalgia cloaks the name of the line that for 77 years was the lifeline to the North. Every once in a while an old stateroom key is returned in the mail to the Skinner Corporation's offices. Sometimes someone writes, enclosing a clipping of an advertisement from an out-dated travel magazine and requesting a brochure. The ads used to say, "When you think Alaska think Alaska Steam," and some people still do. Occasionally a note in shaky handwriting tells of a honeymoon couple who made the trip on the Alaska Line, and wants to do it over again for a golden wedding anniversary celebration.

After the farewell announcement, the Seattle news magazine *Argus* published a tribute to the Alaska Line, lauding "the noble attempt to prevail against the short season, poor haul back, miniscule ports, ceaseless baiting by Governor Gruening, an unsuccessful suit citing restraint of trade, and an aging fleet that poor profits could not allow to be replaced."

That is a suitable epitaph to mark the end of a gallant era, when ships and sailors braved the northern seas to serve the people of Alaska.

The train ship *Alaska III*.

The Ships of the Line

1895 to 1971

Name	Year Built	Gross Tons	Remarks
WILLAPA	1882	337	Purchased 1895, ex GENERAL MILES. Wrecked 1897, later salvaged and renamed BELLINGHAM, burned 1950.
ROSALIE	1893	319	Purchased 1897. Sold 1900, burned 1918.
DIRIGO	1898	843	Purchased 1899. Sank 1914.
FARALLON	1888	750	Purchased 1899. Wrecked 1910.
DOLPHIN	1892	824	Purchased 1900, ex AL FOSTER, THE FOSTER. Sold 1917 and later reported as Chilean gunboat.
JEFFERSON	1904	1,615	Scrapped 1925.

In 1908 the Northwestern Steamship Co. was consolidated with the Alaska Steamship Co. and furnished the following vessels for the new fleet. Dates show when acquired by Northwestern.

Name	Year Built	Gross Tons	Remarks
OLYMPIA	1883	2,837	Purchased 1904, ex DUNBAR CASTLE. Wrecked 1910.
VICTORIA	1870	3,868	Purchased 1904, ex PARTHIA. Sold 1954, converted to barge, scrapped.
DORA	1880	320	Purchased 1905. Sold 1918, wrecked 1920.
OAKLAND	1905	146	Sold 1911, wrecked 1912.
SANTA ANA	1900	1,059	Purchased 1905. Sold 1923, burned 1939.
SANTA CLARA	1900	1,588	Purchased 1905, ex JOHN S. KIMBALL, ex JAMES DOLLAR. Sold 1909, wrecked 1915.
EDITH	1882	2,369	Purchased 1905, ex GLENOCHIL. Foundered 1915.
PENNSYLVANIA	1872	3,343	Purchased 1905. Sold 1909, burned 1918.
OHIO	1873	3,488	Purchased 1909. Wrecked 1909.
SARATOGA	1878	2,820	Purchased 1906. Wrecked 1908.
NORTHWESTERN	1889	3,094	Purchased 1906. Sold 1940, bombed 1942.

Name	Year Built	Gross Tons	Remarks
YUCATAN	1890	3,525	Purchased 1906. Wrecked 1910, later salvaged, sold and renamed SHINKAI MARU.
SEWARD	1907	3,390	Sold 1916, torpedoed 1917.

The following vessels were added to the combined fleet after 1908.

Name	Year Built	Gross Tons	Remarks
LATOUCHE	1910	2,159	Sold 1940.
ALAMEDA	1883	3,158	Purchased 1910. Burned 1931.
MARIPOSA	1883	3,158	Purchased 1911. Wrecked 1917.
CORDOVA	1912	2,273	Purchased on stocks, to have been named CALIFORNIA. Sold 1947. renamed LEE KUNG.
ALASKA(I)	1889	3,309	Purchased 1915, ex KANSAS CITY. Wrecked 1921.
REDONDO	1902	679	Purchased 1915. Sold 1935, reduced to barge, sank 1947.
VALDEZ	1908	2,308	Purchased 1915, ex BENNINGTON. Sold 1923, renamed BROCKTON and scrapped after World War II.
JUNEAU	1908	2,382	Purchased 1915, ex BURLINGTON. Sold 1923, renamed BACK BAY and scrapped after World War II.
KETCHIKAN	1899	2,373	Purchased 1916, ex EUREKA. 1926 renamed NIZINA.
NIZINA			Scrapped 1937.
HENRY T. SCOTT	1913	1,596	Purchased 1916. Sold 1920, sunk in collision 1922.
SKAGWAY	1908	1,838	Purchased 1917, ex STANLEY DOLLAR. Sold 1923, burned 1929.
KENNECOTT	1921	3,620	Wrecked 1923.
ODUNA	1920	3,474	Purchased 1922, ex MEDON. Requisitioned by U.S. government 1944 and turned over to U.S.S.R. as VISHERA. Returned, sold 1948, renamed MARY OLSON.
TANANA(I)	1920	3,474	Purchased 1922, ex DELROSA. Requisitioned by U.S. government 1944 and turned over to U.S.S.R. as POLINA OSPENSKO.
LAKE GEBHARDT	1919	2,810	Purchased 1923. Wrecked 1923 on delivery trip.
NABESNA(I)	1919	2,451	Purchased 1923, ex LAKE FILBERT. Sold 1928 and later renamed ANGOULEME.
ALASKA(II)	1923	4,653	Sold 1955, renamed MAZATLAN, scrapped.
YUKON	1899	5,863	Purchased 1924, ex MEXICO, ex COLON. Wrecked 1946.
DENALI(I)	1920	3,333	Purchased 1925, ex JEPTHA. Wrecked 1935.
DEPERE	1920	3,475	Purchased 1925. Requisitioned by U.S. government 1944 and turned over to U.S.S.R. as TSIOLKOVSKI.
DERBLAY	1920	3,475	Purchased 1926. Sold 1946, renamed YU CHANG, later EASTERN MARINER. Scrapped 1959.

Name	Year Built	Gross Tons	Remarks
LAKINA	1913	2,059	Purchased 1926, ex OLIVER J. OLSON, ex EL CAPITAN. Sold 1947, renamed PING HSING, later NOR' BAY.
ALEUTIAN(I)	1898	5,708	Purchased 1927, ex HAVANA, ex PANAMA. Wrecked 1929.
ALEUTIAN(II)	1906	6,361	Purchased 1930, ex MEXICO. Sold 1954, renamed TRADEWIND. Scrapped.
DELLWOOD	1919	3,923	Purchased 1932. Wrecked 1943.
CURACAO	1895	1,548	Purchased 1933. Sold 1939, renamed HELLENIC SKIPPER. Exploded at sea 1940.
KENAI	1904	382	Purchased 1934, ex GENERAL MIFFLIN. Sold 1942 and converted to towboat.
STARR	1912	525	Purchased 1935. Scrapped 1940.
BERING	1918	2,361	Purchased 1936, ex ANNETTE ROLPH, ex ARTHUR J. BALDWIN. Wrecked 1943, hull later recovered and used as breakwater.
BARANOF	1919	4,990	Purchased 1936, ex SANTA ELISA. Scrapped 1955.
MT. McKINLEY	1918	4,861	Purchased 1936, ex SANTA LUISA, ex EL SALVADOR, ex SANTA ANA. Wrecked 1942.
SUTHERLAND	1918	4,716	Purchased 1937. Sold 1946, renamed OKEANOS and wrecked.
COLUMBIA	1907	5,270	Purchased 1937, ex PRESIDENT, ex DOROTHY ALEXANDER. Sold 1946, renamed PORTUGAL, scrapped 1952.
DENALI(II)	1927	4,302	Purchased 1938, ex CARACAS. Sold 1954, renamed CUBA, later SOUTHERN CROSS. Scrapped 1960.
CHENA	1942	7,180	Purchased 1948, ex CHIEF WASHAKIE. Scrapped 1971.
SUSITNA	1945	3,812	Purchased 1948, ex TERMINAL KNOT. Sold 1969 and scrapped.
NADINA	1944	7,198	Purchased 1950, ex WILLIAM G. LEE, ex DORIAN PRINCE. Scrapped 1970.
ILIAMNA	1944	7,176	Purchased 1951, ex EDMOND MALLET. Scrapped 1972.
TONSINA	1944	7,214	Purchased 1954, ex CHUNG TUNG, ex ADMIRAL ARTHUR P. FAIRFIELD, ex SEACORONET. Scrapped 1970.
GALENA	1945	3,805	Purchased 1955, ex LEVER'S BEND. Scrapped 1972.
FORTUNA	1944	7,210	Purchased 1955, ex SAMUEL L. COBB, ex VOLUNTEER STATE. Scrapped 1971.
TANANA(II)	1945	3,805	Purchased 1956, ex SQUARE KNOT. Sold 1969, scrapped 1970.
TATALINA	1945	3,812	Purchased 1956, ex SQUARE SINNET. Sold 1971, foundered 1979.
NENANA	1944	7,249	Purchased 1959, ex FELIX RIESENBERG, ex TRANSATLANTIC. Scrapped 1971.
TALKEETNA	1944	7,254	Purchased 1959, ex WILLIAM ALLEN WHITE, ex TRANSPACIFIC. Sold 1967 and scrapped.
ODUNA(II)	1945	7,252	Purchased 1964, ex FRANCIS A. RETKA, ex LIBERTY BELL, ex I.R. LASHINS, ex SOUTHPORT. Wrecked 1965.
POLAR PIONEER	1945	3,809	Purchased 1967, ex USN LUCIDOR AF-45. Sold 1972.

Bibliography

Andrews, Ralph. *This Was Seafaring.* Seattle: Superior Publishing Co., 1955.

Balch, Thomas Willing. *The Alaska Frontier.* Caldwell, Idaho: Caxton, 1959.

Bancroft, Hubert Howe. *1730-1885 History of Alaska.* San Francisco: A.L. Bancroft & Co.

Becker, Ethel Anderson. *Klondike '98.* Seattle: Superior Publishing Co., 1960.

Benson, Richard M. *Steamships and Motorships of the West Coast.* 1925.

Brittan, H.B. "The Rise and Fall of Passenger Steamer Service on the Pacific." Unpublished typescript.

Bronson, William. *Still Flying and Nailed to the Mast.* Garden City, New York: Doubleday & Co., 1963.

Bruce, Miner W. *Alaska, Its History and Resources.* Seattle: Lowman & Hanford, 1895.

Burrows, Carl. *Patsy Ann.* Juneau: Self-published, 1939.

Calkins. R.H. *High Tide.* Seattle: Marine Digest Publishing Co., 1936.

Calvin, Jack. *Sitka.* New York: Arrowhead Press, 1890.

Collis, Septima M. *A Woman's Trip to Alaska.* Juneau: Cossell Publishing Co., 1967.

Davidson, George. *Coast Pilot of Alaska.* U.S. Government Printing Office, 1869.

De Armond, R.N. *The Founding of Juneau.* Juneau: Gastineau Channel Centennial Associates, 1967.

Fitch, Edward M. *The Alaska Railroad.* New York: Frederick A. Praeger, 1967.

Gibbs, James. *Disaster Log of Ships.* New York: Bonanza Books, 1971.

Haugland, Mary Lou McMahon. "A History of the Alaska Steamship Co." Thesis. Seattle: University of Washington, 1968.

Hitchman, James B. "A Bibliographical Survey of Pacific Northwest Maritime History in Pacific Northwest." Themes. Edited by James W. Scott. Bellingham, Washington: Western Washington University Center for Pacific Northwest Studies, 1978.

Janson, Lone E. *The Copper Spike.* Edmonds, Washington: Alaska Northwest Publishing Co., 1954.

Kitchener, L.D. *Flag Over the North.* Seattle: Superior Publishing Co., 1954.

Lawson, Will. *Pacific Steamers.* Glasgow: Brown, Son & Ferguson Ltd., 1927.

Mallory, Gwen E., and Iris Shaw. *Two Towels and an Orange.* New York: Comet Press Books, 1955.

Moore, J. Bernard. *Skagway in Days Primeval.* New York: Vantage Press, 1968.

Newell, Gordon. *The H.W. McCurdy Marine History of the Pacific Northwest 1966-1975.* Seattle: Superior Publishing Co., 1977.

Newell, Gordon. *S.O.S. North Pacific.* Portland: Binfords & Mort, 1955.

Newell, Gordon, and Joe **Williamson**. *Pacific Coastal Liners.* Seattle: **Superior** Publishing Co., 1959.

Rogers, Fred. *Shipwrecks of British Columbia.* Vancouver, British Columbia: J.J. Douglas Ltd., 1976.

Sayre, J. Willis. *The Early Waterfront of Seattle.* Reprint. Seattle: Shorey Facsimile, 1971.

Scidmore, R. Ruhamah. *Journeys in Alaska.* Boston: D. Lathrop & Co., 1885.

Shiels, Archie W. Manuscript. Seattle: University of Washington library.

Tourville, Elsie A. *Alaska Bibliography 1570-1970.* Boston: G.K. Hall & Co., 1974.

Wickersham, James. *A Bibliography of Alaskan Literature.* Cordova: *Cordova Daily Times,* 1927.

Williamson, Joe, and James Gibbs. *Maritime Memories of Puget Sound.* Seattle: Superior Publishing Co., 1976.

Wright, E.W. *Lewis and Dryden's Marine History of the Pacific Northwest.* Portland: Lewis & Dryden Ptg. Co., 1895.

Newspaper Files and Periodical Sources

Alaskan, Cordova, 1908-10
The Alaskan, Sitka
Alaska Daily Dispatch, 1899-1901, 1920
Alaska Journal
Alaska Mining Record
Alaska News, Juneau, 1894

Alaska Searchlight, June 26, 1897

Alaska Sportsman, August 1948

Alaska Yukon Magazine, May 1910,
   November 1920

Anchorage Times, 1944-66

Bayers, L.H., index file, scrapbooks and
   albums, Alaska State Library, Juneau

Biography file, University of Washington
   Library

Juneau Mining Record, 1892-98

Marine Digest, March 9, 1963; Sept. 19,
   1944; Sept. 23, 1944; February 1946;
   March 1948

Puget Sound Maritime Historical Society
   News Letter, April 1961

Salmon Fisheries of the Pacific Coast,
   Government Printing Office, 1911

Sea Chest, Puget Sound Maritime Historical
   Society Quarterly, September 1967 to
   date

Seattle Post-Intelligencer, Nov. 18. 1894;
   1895-97

Seattle Times, May 1968; Oct. 16, 1901;
   1910, 1915, 1917

Skagway News, 1899, 1900

Steamboat Bill, December 1954 and March
   1955, Barrington, Rhode Island

U.S. Department of Commerce, 1916,
   Wire-Drag Work in Alaska

Valdez News, November 1901-2

Wrangell Sentinel, May 13, 1915, through
   Aug. 5, 1915

*Sailing Directions and Coast Pilots for
   Alaska and British Columbia*, issued by
   the British, Canadian and U.S.
   governments.

Lucile Saunders McDonald, born in Portland and trained in journalism at the University of Oregon, began her writing career during World War I on newspapers in western Oregon. After the war she went as a free-lance journalist to Mexico, then Central and South America, and eventually joined the staff of the *Buenos Aires Herald* and became United Press night editor for all of South America.

From Buenos Aires she went to New York City, worked for UP, then the Standard News Association, did some magazine writing, and was married. After marriage she fitted her career to her husband's, which took her back to the West Coast, to Cordova, where she was news editor of the *Cordova Daily Times* and correspondent for the Associated Press and *Pacific Fisherman*, then to various parts of Europe with headquarters in Istanbul. There she was a *New York Times* correspondent and, having become a mother, she turned some of her creative energy to writing juvenile books.

Back on the West Coast during World War II, Mrs. McDonald began her 23-year tenure with the *Seattle Times Sunday Magazine,* with regional history as her primary interest.

Mrs. McDonald is coauthor of 12 books and, with publication of *ALASKA STEAM,* the author of 18 more.

Menu covers from the SS *Yukon,* **1937.**

Alaska Geographic Back Issues

The North Slope, Vol. 1, No. 1. The charter issue of *ALASKA GEOGRAPHIC*. Out of print.

One Man's Wilderness, Vol. 1, No. 2. The story of a dream shared by many, fulfilled by a few; a man goes into the Bush, builds a cabin and shares his incredible wilderness experience. Color photos. 116 pages, $9.95.

Admiralty . . . Island in Contention, Vol. 1, No. 3. An intimate and multifaceted view of Admiralty; it's geological and historical past, its present-day geography, wildlife and sparse human population. Color photos. 78 pages, $5.

Fisheries of the North Pacific: History, Species, Gear & Processes, Vol. 1, No. 4. Out of print. (Book edition available)

The Alaska-Yukon Wild Flowers Guide, Vol. 2, No. 1. Out of print. (Book edition available)

Richard Harrington's Yukon, Vol. 2, No. 2. Out of print.

Prince William Sound, Vol. 2, No. 3. Out of print.

Yakutat: The Turbulent Crescent, Vol. 2, No. 4. Out of print.

Glacier Bay: Old Ice, New Land, Vol. 3, No. 1. The expansive wilderness of southeastern Alaska's Glacier Bay National Monument (recently proclaimed a national park and preserve) unfolds in crisp text and color photographs. Records the flora and fauna of the area, its natural history, with hike and cruise information, plus a large-scale color map. 132 pages, $11.95.

The Land: Eye of the Storm, Vol. 3, No. 2. Out of print.

Richard Harrington's Antarctic, Vol. 3, No. 3. The Canadian photojournalist guides readers through remote and little understood regions of the Antarctic and subantarctic. More than 200 color photos and a large fold-out map. 104 pages, $8.95.

The Silver Years of the Alaska Canned Salmon Industry: An Album of Historical Photos, Vol. 3, No. 4. Out of print.

Alaska's Volcanoes: Northern Link in the Ring of Fire, Vol. 4, No. 1. Out of print.

The Brooks Range: Environmental Watershed, Vol. 4, No. 2. Out of print.

Kodiak: Island of Change, Vol. 4, No. 3. Out of print.

Wilderness Proposals: Which Way for Alaska's Lands? Vol. 4, No. 4. Out of print.

Cook Inlet Country, Vol. 5, No. 1. Out of print. All-new edition (Vol. 10, No. 2) available.

Southeast: Alaska's Panhandle, Vol. 5, No. 2. Explores southeastern Alaska's maze of fjords and islands, mossy forests and glacier-draped mountains — from Dixon Entrance to Icy Bay, including all of the state's fabled Inside Passage. Along the way are profiles of every town, together with a look at the region's history, economy, people, attractions and future. Includes large fold-out map and seven area maps. 192 pages, $12.95.

Bristol Bay Basin, Vol. 5, No. 3. Out of print.

Alaska Whales and Whaling, Vol. 5, No. 4. The wonders of whales in Alaska — their life cycles, travels and travails — are examined, with an authoritative history of commercial and subsistence whaling in the North. Includes a fold-out poster of 14 major whale species in Alaska in perspective, color photos and illustrations, with historical photos and line drawings. 144 pages, $12.95.

Yukon-Kuskokwim Delta, Vol. 6, No. 1. Out of print.

The Aurora Borealis, Vol. 6, No. 2. The northern lights — in ancient times seen as a dreadful forecast of doom, in modern days an inspiration to countless poets. What causes the aurora, how it works, and how and why scientists are studying it today and its implications for our future. 96 pages, $7.95.

Alaska's Native People, Vol. 6, No. 3. Examine the varied worlds of the Inupiat Eskimo, Yup'ik Eskimo, Athabascan, Aleut, Tlingit, Haida and Tsimshian. Included are sensitive, informative articles by Native writers, plus a large, four-color map detailing the Native villages and defining the language areas, 304 pages, $24.95.

The Stikine, Vol. 6, No. 4. River route to three Canadian gold strikes in the 1800s, the Stikine is the largest and most navigable of several rivers that flow from northwestern Canada through southeastern Alaska on their way to the sea. Illustrated with contemporary color photos and historic black-and-white; includes a large fold-out map. 96 pages, $9.95.

Alaska's Great Interior, Vol. 7, No. 1. Alaska's rich Interior country, west from the Alaska-Yukon Territory border and including the huge drainage between the Alaska Range and the Brooks Range, is covered thoroughly. Included are the region's people, communities, history, economy, wilderness areas and wildlife. Illustrated with contemporary color and black-and-white photos. Includes a large fold-out map. 128 pages, $9.95.

A Photographic Geography of Alaska, Vol. 7, No. 2. An overview of the entire state — a visual tour through the six regions of Alaska: Southeast, Southcentral/Gulf Coast, Alaska Peninsula and Aleutians, Bering Sea Coast, Arctic and Interior. Plus a handy appendix of valuable information — "Facts About Alaska." Revised in 1983. Approximately 160 color and black-and-white photos and 35 maps. 192 pages, $15.95.

The Aleutians, Vol. 7, No. 3. Home of the Aleut, a tremendous wildlife spectacle, a major World War II battleground and now the heart of a thriving new commercial fishing industry. Contemporary color and black-and-white photographs, and a large fold-out map. 224 pages, $14.95.

Klondike Lost: A Decade of Photographs by Kinsey & Kinsey, Vol. 7, No. 4. An album of rare photographs and all-new text about the lost Klondike boom town of Grand Forks, second in size only to Dawson during the gold rush. $12.95.

Wrangell-Saint Elias, Vol. 8, No. 1. Mountains, including the continent's second- and fourth-highest peaks, dominate this international wilderness that sweeps from the Wrangell Mountains in Alaska to the southern Saint Elias range in Canada. Includes a large fold-out map. 144 pages, $9.95.

Alaska Mammals, Vol. 8, No. 2. From tiny ground squirrels to the powerful polar bear, and from the tundra to the magnificent whales inhabiting Alaska's waters, this volume includes 80 species of mammals found in Alaska. 184 pages, $12.95.

The Kotzebue Basin, Vol. 8, No. 3. Examines northwestern Alaska's thriving trading area of Kotzebue Sound and the Kobuk and Noatak river basins, lifelines of the region's Inupiat Eskimos, early explorers, and present-day, hardy residents. 184 pages, $12.95.

Alaska National Interest Lands, Vol. 8, No. 4. Following passage of the bill formalizing Alaska's national interest land selections (d-2 lands), longtime Alaskans Celia Hunter and Ginny Wood review each selection, outlining location, size, access, and briefly describing the region's special attractions. 242 pages, $14.95.

Alaska's Glaciers, Vol. 9, No. 1. Examines in depth the massive rivers of ice, their composition, exploration, present-day distribution and scientific significance. 144 pages, $9.95.

Sitka and Its Ocean/Island World, Vol. 9, No. 2. From the elegant capital of Russian America to a beautiful but modern port, Sitka, on Baranof Island, has become a commercial and cultural center for southeastern Alaska. 128 pages, $9.95.

Islands of the Seals: The Pribilofs, Vol. 9, No. 3. Great herds of northern fur seals drew Russians and Aleuts to these remote Bering Sea islands where they founded permanent communities and established a unique international commerce. 128 pages, $9.95.

Alaska's Oil/Gas & Minerals Industry, Vol. 9, No. 4. Experts detail the geological processes and resulting mineral and fossil fuel resources that are now in the forefront of Alaska's economy. Illustrated with historical black-and-white and contemporary color photographs. 216 pages, $12.95.

Adventure Roads North: The Story of the Alaska Highway and Other Roads in *The MILEPOST*, Vol. 10, No. 1. From Alaska's first highway — the Richardson — to the famous Alaska Highway, first overland route to the 49th state, text and photos provide a history of Alaska's roads and take a mile-by-mile look at the country they cross. 224 pages, $14.95.

ANCHORAGE and the Cook Inlet Basin, Vol. 10, No. 2. "Anchorage country" . . . the Kenai, the Susitna Valley, and Matanuska. Heavily illustrated in color and including three illustrated maps . . . one an uproarious artist's forecast of "Anchorage 2035." 168 pages, $14.95.

Alaska's Salmon Fisheries, Vol. 10, No. 3. The work of *ALASKA* magazine Outdoors Editor Jim Rearden, this issue takes a comprehensive look at Alaska's most valuable commercial fishery. 128 pages, $12.95.

Up the Koyukuk, Vol. 10, No. 4. Highlights the Koyukuk region of north-central Alaska . . . the wildlife, fauna, Native culture and more. 152 pages. $14.95.

Nome: City of the Golden Beaches, Vol. 11, No. 1. The colorful history of Alaska's most famous gold rush town has never been told like this before. Illustrated with hundreds of rare black-and-white photos, the book traces the story of Nome from the crazy days of the 1900 gold rush. 184 pages, $14.95.

Alaska's Farms and Gardens, Vol. 11, No. 2. An overview of the past, present, and future of agriculture in Alaska, and a wealth of information on how to grow your own fruit and vegetables in the north. 144 pages, $12.95.

Chilkat River Valley, Vol. 11, No. 3. This issue explores the mountain-rimmed valley at the head of the Inside Passage, its natural resources, and those hardy residents who make their home along the Chilkat. 112 pages, $12.95.

NEXT ISSUE:
The Northwest Territories, Vol. 12, No. 1. This issues takes an in-depth look at Canada's immense Northwest Territories, which comprises some of the most beautiful and isolated land in North America. Supervising editor Richard Harrington has brought together informative text and color photos covering such topics as geology and mineral resources, prehistoric people, native art, and the search for the Northwest Passage. Also included is a look under the ice of the Canadian Arctic. To members in February 1985. Price to be announced.

Your $30 membership in the Alaska Geographic Society includes 4 subsequent issues of *ALASKA GEOGRAPHIC*, the Society's official quarterly. Please add $4 for non-U.S. membership.

Additional membership information available upon request. Single copies of the *ALASKA GEOGRAPHIC* back issues are also available. When ordering, please make payments in U.S. funds and add $1 postage/handling per copy. To order back issues send your check or money order and volumes desired to:

The Alaska Geographic Society

Box 4-EEE, Anchorage, Alaska 99509